Are You Ready to... Be Your Own Boss?

Carol Denbow

Plain and Simple Books

NORTH BEND, OREGON

Plain and Simple Books, North Bend, Oregon
Printed by Wegferds' Printing & Publications, North Bend, Oregon
Cover design by Karen Wegfahrt
Edited by Cori Ashley

ISBN: 0-937861-69-3

Publisher's Cataloging-in-Publication Data

Denbow, Carol.
    Are you ready to be your own boss? / Carol Denbow.
    p. cm.
    Includes index.
    ISBN 0-937861-69-3

1. Entrepreneurship. 2. Success in business. 3. New business
enterprises. 4. Business planning. 5. Self-employed. I. Title.

HD62.5 D45 2006
658.041—dc22   2006903382

Manufactured in the United States of America
10 9 8 7 6 5 4 3 2

*Dedicated to my husband Craig, without whose
tremendous support and continuous encouragement,
I never would have finished writing this book.
I love you too much!*

Acknowledgments

Though I did write this book, and my name is on the cover, I am not comfortable taking the full credit for it. I would like to thank the following individuals who graciously shared their business and personal experiences with me. Without their invaluable input, this book would not have been written.

Thank you Pete Lawson, Flarry and Joan Marangio, my good friends James and Sandra Flanagan, Jim Pionke, my best friend Maria Aarvig, Joe Benetti, Abigail Ashworth, Dan and Roberta Abel, Lee Wright, Scott Farlow, and Rick Gitchen for taking time out of your extremely busy schedules to sit with me for an interview for which you got paid zip.

Thank you Roy Metzger for your very expensive expert advice that you shared with me for free.

I would also like to thank my mom and dad for teaching me the value of every dollar earned, which you also did for free.

Thank you Robert Stevenson for sharing your insight on customer service.

Thank you Elleta Nolte for inspiring me to keep writing until it was done.

Thank you Cori Ashley for editing this book and fixing my boo-boos.

A special thanks to my kids, Justin and Jennifer, for putting up with my long hours at my business and always being patient with me. I love you both more than life.

Table of Contents

Introduction

If you want your new business to succeed, you *must* know why most new businesses fail to be successful. Most people spend more time planning their vacations than they do their new business. Most small business books won't tell you the poor odds for success. They want to get you all pumped up on your "rags to riches" dream. My intention isn't to scare you away from your dream, but to inform you about the odds of failure that are a reality that most people starting out choose to ignore. This book will help you beat those odds.

My plan is to alert you to the reality of what it will take for you to have a successful business. The commitment you need is far more than most people are aware of. No amount of business education classes at the local college can fully prepare you for the day you step out into the real world of small business ownership. There are hundreds of books on small business, and they all can be very helpful to you. But the truth is, most of them don't address many of the common problems that occur in new businesses. Sometimes things just don't go "by the book." Trust me when I say, in new businesses, things *never* go by the book. They won't even go completely by this book.

What I won't do is try to dazzle you with $10 words. I also won't be teaching you any specific business plan. What I will do is try to show you some of the misconceptions we all have, and mistakes we all make that can cause delays to our business success. I believe that if you are aware of these, you will avoid them better and in turn will more likely be able to move your business forward to a successful level.

Are You Ready to Be Your Own Boss contains success and failure stories from real people like you. Those people will share their experiences, good and bad. My hope is that you will have a better chance of success by reading about their trials and avoiding the mistakes they have made.

After you've read about the truth and consequences of self-employment, and if you are still willing to take the risk, then I suggest you go out and choose a book with a more typical step-by-step mechanical guide on starting a new business. I will provide you with the names of some good books. If after you have read this book you choose not to take the gamble, don't feel bad — most people just aren't suited for self-employment, and it's good to recognize that before you commit.

I wish everyone success in all aspects of their lives.

My Own Story
"For the Love of Horses"

I drove into the ranch bright and early on Halloween day, 1986. There it was, mostly deserted and half torn down or collapsed. But I had waited eagerly for this moment and I was sure I could do this. I wanted it bad!

I parked the car — yes I said car, not truck. Yet I had just poured all of our savings and some borrowed money into purchasing a horse-boarding ranch, and I didn't even own a truck. Other than a quick peek around two months earlier, I hadn't really looked at the place before. I was buying a county land lease with some horse corrals, not a successful business, and even though this ranch was originally opened in 1976 and had seen its heyday, those days were long past.

The sellers had given me one "office" key. I approached the so-called office to find that the office key wasn't to a normal door lock, but rather to a padlock on the door. So I unlocked it and took the lock off the latch. The door wouldn't open until I lifted the whole door and shoved it inward. When the dust settled, I saw a metal desk with a rusty folding chair tucked under it. On the desk was an old recipe box and a rotary phone in desperate need of cleaning before I would have ever put my mouth near the receiver. That was about all there was. The office building — really an old eight-by-twelve-foot shed — was constructed with the roof holding the walls up, instead of the walls holding the roof up, and the center of the roof was sagging. There was a large window above the desk, and a small broken window on the other side of the door. Outside the door there was a porch cover. The supports for the cover were so weak that if you leaned on one, it would flex. So, of course, nobody was ever allowed to lean on it. The floor was once made up of plywood, but was worn down to the dirt.

From there I didn't know what to do, so I opened the recipe box. Inside were the names of boarders who kept their horses at the ranch. Along with their names, were months of the year with dollar amounts paid to the ranch for boarding fees. There were around twenty cards in the box, but there were only seven horses outside in corrals. I had no idea who those seven horses belonged to, so I went out to explore. There were about twenty-five corrals, in most of which the structure had rusted or broken. The ground under the covered areas of the corrals and between them was lower than the outside areas. As quickly as I noticed this, it began to rain.

It rained for two weeks straight, without any real break. The corrals flooded and quickly turned to muck. When I finally figured out who those seven horses belonged to, the owners showed up with trailers to relocate their horses to a better, dryer boarding ranch. That was how things began. I was no longer sure I could do this, and didn't know if I even wanted to try. How did I get myself into this?

"Can You Make It?"

It's very important that while you're reading this book you take mental and written notes on some important issues. Most everything you read here will apply in one form or another to your particular business. You picked up this book to help you, so use it. Get a highlighter, pencil, or pen to underline or just take notes as you go along. Staying focused is very important in any business. This book itself is a business for me. I have a large chart in my view at all times when I am writing. The chart lists important things I need to stay focused on. The chart helps me stay on track regarding what I am writing about. You can make your own chart to remind yourself daily of your business plan. Staying focused on your business plan will help direct you through the steps you need to take to start and operate a successful business.

Statistically Speaking
— Odds Of Success —

So your plan is to give up your job and start a new business of your own. What will that take? What will be your new responsibilities? Probably more than you planned. The first thing you need to completely understand is that you will be giving up your job security and many of the benefits that come with it.

When you leave your *real* job for self-employment, there will no longer be any company paid sick or vacation days. If you had received free or low cost health insurance through your employer, it will now be up to you to pay the entire cost. Individual insurance is always more expensive than group plans, so your cost will be higher than your employer's.

Retirement benefits, savings plans, profit sharing, and all company organized financial plans will be left behind. You will be responsible for setting up and contributing to your own savings and retirement. Being responsible for your own financial future can be challenging. It takes a great deal of personal commitment and self-control.

Rick Gitchen was a practicing attorney with a guaranteed income and benefits. He left his practice and joined his brother Dan to open a coffee house in Chino Hills, California in 1994.

> Rick Gitchen, Seattle's Best Coffee®, Chino Hills, California — Security is the biggest thing you give up. The idea of having a paycheck in the same amount you can count on every week is gone. The benefits

you get now, your insurance, or whatever it is that you count on is gone. For me, that was the most difficult thing to give up in favor of the unsure return every month.

Self-employed people find they have many new responsibilities after leaving their previous jobs.

I drove into a new housing development to meet with Dan Abel, owner of AD Construction and Remodel for an interview for this book. Dan has been in the construction business for over thirty years.

Dan Abel, AD Construction and Remodel, Coos Bay, Oregon — When you work for someone else you have set responsibilities, when you work for yourself, you are responsible for everything.

I remember when I worked for someone else, I would work so many hours. I would stay late when they asked me to, come in on my day off when they called, or work whenever they needed extra help. I just wanted to be a good employee, and boy did I love those paychecks every Thursday!

One day someone very special to me said, "You should be in your own business." He said that if I put that much energy into a job working for someone else, imagine how much energy I could put into my own business. Put all that energy into making money for me instead of somebody else. That's when I decided I wanted to be self-employed. It wasn't a lifetime dream for me, it just happened. Until then, I *thought* I had worked long hours at my job. I never realized what was in store for me.

As it turned out, I needed all that energy and more. Because of my lack of planning, I wasted hours, days, and months learning things the hard way. I quickly found out there was not going to be any Thursday paychecks and I hadn't really planned things out. I worked many *free* hours.

I want to talk about your odds of success so that you know up front that small business success is a lot harder to achieve than most people realize. I feel it's very important you know the truth and consequences of self-employment so you'll know what you'll be up against to better prepare for the struggles ahead.

The myth that nine out of ten businesses close in their first year may or may not be completely true. According to more recent Dun and Bradstreet data, 76 percent of new companies were still in business after two years, 47 percent after four years, and 38 percent after six years. These estimates are substantially different than what is still commonly believed. Personally, I believe from the interviews I have done with business owners that many of those 38 percent still in business after six years are continually struggling and are still not guaranteed permanent success.

These business survival statistics are based on the number of new business licenses applied for each year, which are not renewed in following years. The licenses could be for a person selling crafts at the swap meet on Saturdays, or someone in a temporary business, or just as a tax shelter. Some of these "failed" businesses could have been sold or transferred to another individual. These estimates are hard to prove either way. But the fact remains: the majority of new businesses are destined for failure, be it after one, or even after six years.

Statistically, more men are self-employed than are women. Women may be selling themselves short in the business world. Although times have changed, society has taught us in the past that men are leaders. All of our past presidents have been men. Women need to realize that starting a business requires attention to detail, devotion, commitment, and nurturing, all of which are natural characteristics of themselves. Women make great entrepreneurs, but the business failure rate is equally sexed.

Studies show businesses that do survive longer had more cash up front to invest. Other survival factors include the owner's age, higher education, and previous experience in their field. According to a 2002 United States Census Bureau report, most business owners are between the ages of thirty-five and sixty-four and have had ten to nineteen years of work experience prior to self-employment. More experience in life and business seem to translate into more competent decision-making.

There are many reasons for failure. Out of 13,000 failed businesses surveyed, these were the main reasons listed for closure.

- Lack of planning
- Inability to manage money
- Inability to manage employees
- Not enough money
- Neglect
- Fraud
- Lack of experience
- Mismanagement
- Poor cash flow or low sales

Some businesses fail because the owner lacks certain human qualities necessary for success. I read one business book that had a list of thirty human qualities needed for success. The author stated that if you had a certain percentage of these thirty qualities you would be successful. When I read the list, I felt *all* were necessary for any kind of success in life, especially in business. I have my own list below. If you don't possess *all* of these qualities, you will not succeed — period! So start checking off.

[   ] You have energy and good health

[   ] You are a self-starter

[   ] You have a willingness to work hard

[   ] You are a good organizer

[   ] You are able to make decisions

[   ] You are able to make plans and follow through

[   ] You are able to inspire and direct others

[   ] You are honest

[   ] You are a jack of all trades and a master at one!

Ask yourself these other questions, and be honest with yourself — it doesn't help you to lie to a book! How do you keep your own personal finances? Do you balance your checkbook regularly? Do you have credit card debt? Loans? How you manage your personal finances is a good sign of how you will manage your business finances.

It's easier to be successful if you're motivated to work for someone else — there's a guaranteed paycheck every week. Working for a paycheck usually means there will be someone to give you direction and instructions on how to complete a job; someone who sticks their boot in your ass to get you going. But when you require your own boot, in your own ass, it's harder to get that "kick."

Maria Aarvig is a partner in a major law firm with three locations in Southern California.

> Maria Aarvig, Creason and Aarvig, LLC, attorneys, Riverside, California — When things go bad, the buck's going to stop at your desk. You're going to lie awake at night worrying about whether your employees are covered or whether you paid for your inventory. Those things are all going to be on you. It's going to be a lot of hard work.

Are you ready for the challenges of starting your own business? Take the quiz on the following pages. Answer the questions honestly. Then retake the quiz at the end of this book and see if the answers are the same.

Yes   No

[   ]   [   ] Do I have enough cash to invest (other than necessary household income)?

List where your business assets will be coming from:

[   ]   [   ] Do I have enough household income or savings to get me through the first year?

Where is your monthly household income coming from?

[   ]   [   ] Am I good with my personal financial management?

List any late payments you've had in the past five years:

[   ]   [   ] Will I have medical insurance for my family and myself?

Where will it come from and what will the cost be?

[   ]   [   ] Am I in good health?

When was your last physical?

[   ]   [   ] Do I have adequate knowledge or education in the business field I am choosing?

List all experience and education:

Yes   No

[   ]   [   ] Is there room in the market I have chosen for additional competitors?

Who is your competition?

[   ]   [   ] Do I have unlimited time to invest?

What are your other commitments?

[   ]   [   ] Do I have patience?

Ask your spouse or mother!

[   ]   [   ] Does my family support me in this business venture, 100 percent?

List any who are skeptical:

[   ]   [   ] Do I get along well with other people?

[   ]   [   ] Am I committed to and excited about this business venture?

Time to Get to Work
— Time Commitment —

The misconception of self-employment is the commitment of time. While it was raining for two weeks, I assumed there was nothing for me to do at my ranch. I was self-employed now. I could set my own hours, and my time didn't include rainy days. I found myself going out to get breakfast, or lunch, or whatever! One day, I was sitting in the local café and it hit me; I might not — no, I *will* not — succeed by sitting in a café watching the rain come down. That's the day I went to work (in the rain, of course).

According to a United States Census Bureau survey of business owners, 51 percent will work over 336 days per year. 34.5 percent will work over 40 hours per week and 13.6 percent of those will work more than 60 hours per week.

Lee Wright and Jim Dalhover had owned and operated Commonwealth Upholstery for forty years. Only weeks after our interview, Lee passed away from a rare form of cancer. He had worked that day, and planned to go to work the next day. He will be missed.

> Lee Wright, Commonwealth Upholstery, Fullerton, California — Each of us has only missed seven days of work in our forty years of business.

For only thirteen months Scott Farlow has owned and operated a Sears in North Bend, Oregon. He worked for Sears prior to that for twenty years.

> Scott Farlow, Fambiz, Inc., dba Sears, North Bend, Oregon — I put in between sixty-five and seventy-five hours a week and it's a lot of work. But at the end of the day it's much more rewarding than working for someone else. My store is in the top ten in the nation in volume. The only way to make it successful is to really work hard at it. I think one of the reasons we're doing so well is because I'm there every day. I'm on the sales floor, I'm talking and joking with customers, I'm just in it.

Abigail Ashworth has owned two hair salons in Coos Bay, Oregon over a period of thirteen years.

> Abigail Ashworth, Personal Touch Of Hair Design, Coos Bay, Oregon — Working for yourself, you should work until the daily work is done. That's how you get your new clientele; that's how you build clientele.

The myth is, when you're self-employed, you can set and work your own hours.

The truth is, sometimes new business failure is directly related to the business owner failing, up front,

to recognize how much time will be involved with his or her new venture.

Have you ever heard anyone talk of the importance of "owner presence?" How many hours do you think Bill Gates worked to get Microsoft where it is today?

> Maria Aarvig, Creason and Aarvig, LLC, attorneys, Riverside, California — It's not going to be nine to five. It's not going to be Monday through Friday.

Do you realize that the average business owner/manager will receive about 190 messages a day? It takes a lot of time just to listen to that many messages, and much longer to respond to them. What you will need to succeed is the commitment of your time, all you have. Looking back, I hear haunting echoes of naïve people, including myself, saying, "I want to be my own boss and work whenever I want." What a bunch of crap! You will have to commit to what will seem like endless hours and sleepless nights. Forget about weekends and holidays, you'll most likely be working them. Vacations, did you say? Not a chance. Maybe somewhere down the road there will be time. But for new business owners, time is your most necessary commodity. If you are not willing to give your time unconditionally, put this book away and go back to your nine to five security blanket, collect your paycheck on Friday, and hit Vegas for the weekend, because if you don't have the time, you're not going to succeed.

Dan Abel, AD Construction and Remodel, LLC, Coos Bay, Oregon — Working for someone else is a set forty-hour workweek. Working for yourself, double that and double that again. You seem to work pretty much 24/7. Time management is one of the biggest differences between working for someone else and working for yourself. When you work for yourself, if you don't know how to manage your time, you'll never get anything done. I've seen so many people who have been employed for many years decide they want to become self-employed because they think they'll have a lot of free time. Then they find out that they don't have any free time and, in fact, they don't even have their weekends anymore.

Joe Benetti started a small deli in 1979 with no restaurant experience. A few years later he converted the deli into a beautiful Italian restaurant.

Joe Benetti, Benetti's Italian Restaurant, Coos Bay, Oregon — Even today, after being in business for twenty-six years, it should be fewer hours, but it's not.

If you want to start a business, but you need to continue working another job, the chances for your new business's success lessen, unless you are only looking for a part-time business venture. For a new full-time career being self-employed, your best odds are always to have unlimited time to invest. Some people are able to manage enough time in each day to keep that regular job afloat. But I would recommend starting fresh without that obstacle. If that's not an option for you, choose your new business wisely. Keep in mind what hours you can make available, and choose a venture that will not require as much time involvement. I still stress the importance of time investment; if it's not there, you narrow your chances of success.

Jim and Pam Pionke opened their antique store in 1988. Prior to opening their store, antique hunting was their weekend hobby.

> Jim Pionke, Ace and Bubba Treasure Hunters, Racine, Wisconsin — For almost fourteen years, one of us would work at our store and one of us would go out and work another job somewhere else. Our store happened to be next door to a restaurant. My wife used to wait tables there in the afternoons.

In a retail business, such as a store, some people figure to save money they will work the store alone when starting out. That would appear to be a great idea, but have they considered that they might need to go out and pick up products for the store? Products like store merchandise, change for the register, sales books, or even needing to make a trip to the bank. Most of the places they need to go would most likely only be open the same hours as their own store. Now what? Sometimes there just isn't enough time. You might put in twelve-hour days, but still fall short. Plan for these "little" problems. Make sure the time you invest will work for your business.

In other types of retail business, such as mail order, or an Internet business, you can work from your home. This might be a better option for you if time is an issue.

Roberta Abel owns Giftabel.com, an online gift store that she started on her own. Her prior job was as a manager and purchasing agent for an office supply store. Before she started her company, she didn't even own a computer. Giftabel.com gets about 10,000 hits a month.

> Roberta Abel, Giftabel.com, Coos Bay, Oregon — I didn't have the time to have a regular business because I was so busy with raising a child who needed special attention at that time. I needed a way to stay home, so I tried to think of a way to do that and make some supplemental income too. That's when I saw these unique Australian garden pots and figured I could sell them online. Later, I found other great products to add to my online store. Now I sell several gift items. The benefit of a home-based online retail business is that you don't have to be somewhere else at any certain time. The only bad thing about it is it's still hard to get away for more than a few days at a time. If you want to leave for a week, you still have to have someone to take orders and ship the product out.

Joan Marangio is seventy-five years old and operating her own small business in Ontario, California.

> Joan Marangio, F.M. Boutique, Ontario, California — I buy and refurbish antiques and collectables for resale. I rent space to sell my merchandise in a boutique in Upland, California.

Joan doesn't need to be at the boutique all day; she has someone else sell her items. Her time investment is not limited to being in one place all day. This is a good retail business plan for someone who doesn't want to take a huge risk or doesn't have the time due to an existing job or other obligations.

After your business becomes successful, and with good planning, your hours might become more flexible. In your new full-time business, you may even be able to set your own schedule.

> Rick Gitchen, Seattle's Best Coffee®, Chino Hills, California — When you start out, it's 24/7, but the thing I love about self-employment is that now that we're making good profits, I can set my own schedule. I don't live by anyone else's clock and I call my own shots. Of course, as with any business, I still get those calls at five in the morning if something doesn't work in one of the stores, or if someone didn't show up, or if there's some other problem.

Any way you look at it, you must commit your time. Most business failure comes from lack of planning, and time is a big part of what people don't plan for. The Rolling Stones were not all right — time is not "always" on your side.

Spouse, Kids, & the In-Laws — Family Support —

When venturing into a new business career, it is critical to have the full support of your family. Remember, they too have an investment in all this. The time you sink into your new opportunity is time they lose with you.

> Dan Abel, AD Construction and Remodel, LLC, Coos Bay, Oregon — When I was single, I could put in my twelve-hour days and come home dog tired and the only one who would get ticked off at me was my dog. Now that I'm married and have a family, that all changes. My home time is not my own, and it creates quite a stress on my family. My wife would like to have me home by six for dinner and that would be fine in the winter months, but in the summer there's four more hours of daylight. When you're working for someone else you can punch out and go home. You have your evenings and your weekends and everyone is happy and good. But being self-employed, I don't see where I could even begin to pay my bills

and take care of things if I said that at five p.m. each
day I'm not going to stay and work anymore. The
business just requires a tremendous amount of hours.

I truly believe that my previous marriage failed in part
because of my new business, even though it had been my
husband who encouraged me and allowed me to get things
going. He had his own career and was only partly involved
with the business. Just a year or so after buying the business,
I think he felt alone and neglected, and we divorced. Had
we both understood from the onset how much time I would
need to invest for the success of the business, the divorce
may not have occurred.

**The myth is, owning your own business will give
you more time with your family.**

**The truth is, your new business will need constant
nurturing to be successful, and you will have a price
to pay. The price is time, and most often, the time
is away from your family.**

I'm not saying that every new business owner will divorce
or go through tough times at home. I'm just saying that
everyone involved needs to know what time investment
means.

The rest of my family made sacrifices too. I think my mother
began to get irritated after a few years because our family

used to be together for every holiday. After I became self-employed, I could never make it. On Easter Sunday, during my fifth year in business, I promised my mom I would come for Easter dinner. I dressed in a nice white blouse with yellow slacks — typical Easter colors. I stopped by my ranch just to make sure everything was okay before I left for my mom's house. While I was there (for a short ten-minute drop in), one of my customer's horses cut its leg on a wire fence. It was bleeding profusely. Someone had to pinch off the artery and hold it until a veterinarian could get there, and, of course, that someone was me. Bent over, but still on my feet, holding that artery in a white blouse and yellow pants, I lasted about thirty minutes and then finally dropped to my knees into a pool of blood. The vet didn't show up for two hours and my mom's Easter dinner was over. So was mine. Mom wasn't too happy.

I strongly advise that your entire family read this book so they all understand that there will be risks and what they might be giving up. If your family understands the risks clearly, you will avoid the "but I didn't realize" later. I also suggest involving your family in the entire decision-making and planning of your new business: even your mom.

"Choosing Your Business"

Eenie... Meenie... Miney... Mo...
— Pick One —

If you're reading this book, it's because you've already decided that you would like to own your own business, right? This is most likely your first real attempt at self-employment. 65 percent of the business owners out there are first-time owners. Almost 70 percent of new businesses are started from scratch by someone like you.

You probably also have an idea of the type of business you want to start. Keep in mind, some people make bad choices when choosing their business. They only look at the moneymaking side of it. Now I realize, we all want the money, but doesn't your happiness matter too? Remember, this is your real life, not a fantasy. But there is a way you can have the money and happiness too.

Dan Abel, AD Construction and Remodel, LLC, Coos Bay, Oregon — You see so many people doing work that they hate. After work they go home and get their personal satisfaction from their toys or hobbies. Ever since I was a kid, I loved building things and working with my hands. I feel like what I loved to do as a hobby, I get to do for pay.

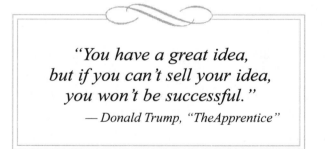

"You have a great idea,
but if you can't sell your idea,
you won't be successful."
— Donald Trump, "TheApprentice"

Let's say there are millions of dollars to be made in the paper industry. Let's say it's an easy business to get into. I will tell you right now, if you don't love the paper industry, you will probably fail, regardless of how easy it is, or how much money you can earn. You need to love what you do to find the greatest success.

The myth is, because you don't like what you do now, you can try *anything* else and you'll better succeed.

The truth is, you have to enjoy what you do in order to succeed at it.

Doesn't it just make more sense when choosing a new livelihood to choose something you enjoy doing?

I have read some books on business that have suggested to *not* look at your hobbies as a business choice, and I strongly disagree. Most other books I researched did agree with me on how to choose your business. If you can't wait until you have time off to do the things you enjoy, don't you think you would enjoy working more if you were doing those things as your job? Now keep in mind, when looking at your hobby as a potential business venture, there is one concern. Don't spend all of your income and profits on your own hobby. Why aren't cocaine dealers rich? Because they blow all their profits! Do you get what I'm saying? No, I'm not suggesting you take up cocaine dealing. Just be careful that you don't use up your income and profits for a fun time with your hobby before you've taken care of business and personal household needs.

A business can be cheap and simple or complicated and expensive to start-up. If you like the outdoors, it could be as simple as buying a mower, edger, and blower and starting a gardening business. You could go out and buy a small flatbed trailer and haul gravel, decorative rock, or topsoil to people's homes. Buy a chainsaw and cut down trees. Buy a vacuum, mop, and some cleansers and start a housekeeping service. There are many options for someone with little to invest. Most of the big companies you know of started out very small.

Flarry and Joan Marangio started their six-million-dollar-a-year business by buying an existing fire extinguisher business. All they got with their purchase was a 1946 pickup truck with a bed full of old trade-in extinguishers. Flarry was a professional firefighter when they bought the business.

> Flarry Marangio, F.M. Chemical, Ontario, California
> — Crawl before you walk. You're not going to succeed
> without having a passion for what you are doing.

Jim Pionke, Ace and Bubba Treasure Hunters, Racine, Wisconsin — If you don't love it, and you're doing it purely for the money, don't do it. If you're doing it purely for the money, you're better off working for someone else. The only way to be successful in a small business is to love what you're doing.

Here are some tips to help you pick your business. First, get your paper out and be prepared to take some notes. Make a list of your hobbies and interests; things you enjoy doing. Then under each one, list all the possible ways to make money with that hobby. Here is an example of what my list would have looked like:

MY HOBBIES AND INTERESTS

GOLF
Operate a golf course
Build golf clubs
Teach golf
Sell golf equipment
Operate a driving range
Open a pro-shop

HORSES
Board horses
Rent horses for trail rides
Tack and supply store
Feed store
Train horses
Teach riding

SEWING
Custom altering
Quilt-making

Sewing machine sales or repair
Sell sewing supplies
Operate a fabric store

I realize there are many more ways to make money off each of these lists; these are just examples. Spend at least a week letting your mind wander and keep your list with you at all times. You will be surprised at what you come up with on your list. Once your list is complete, look through it for any expertise you may have in any one field.

> Dan Abel, AD Construction and Remodel, LLC, Coos Bay, Oregon — Pick a field that you have good sense about and that you've done your research in.

You're always better off with more knowledge than the next guy. Some of the categories on your list might need more education to pursue, and education never hurt anyone. You don't want to lose this opportunity by rushing into something before you're fully prepared.

Where's That Place?
— Location —

With some businesses, location won't matter as much. But with most, it's location, location, and location!

The myth is, the rent is cheaper and will save you money.

The truth is, a bad location can close you down faster than anything.

> Rick Gitchen, Seattle's Best Coffee®, Chino Hills, California — Once we had the business figured out, we knew that the most important thing left was the right location. As we did our research, the thing we saw that differentiated the successful places from the unsuccessful places, for the most part, were their locations. Even if you had a good idea, the right product, the right people, and you made your product with quality, if you were buried in the back of a shopping center, or you were in a place that was difficult to access, or in a neighborhood that couldn't financially support it, you weren't going to succeed.

Location is extremely important in nearly all businesses. You'll need to look into your area for your product's demand. Your product is whatever you're selling: service or merchandise. For instance, I chose horse boarding and horse rentals as my product from my list. For that, I went out and looked for any existing similar businesses in my area. I found the only existing boarding stables were on private property in an area that was, at the time, considered the fastest developing community in the western states. Which meant, in my opinion, those stables were sitting on property that would soon be developed for housing. I also took notes on the quality of the facilities and boarding fees charged at each of those facilities. Most were extremely expensive and catered to high-end clients. I saw a few others that were pretty crappy, to put it in horse terms. So I began from there, researching the operation costs of a mid-level facility. I found a place on county property that could not be developed for homes and it worked out well. Within just a couple of years, most of those other facilities were closed down due to development. I was left being just about the only game in town.

You should try looking within ten miles of your home first; it's a good idea to be as close as possible to your business in the event of any emergency or problems. Do research for the supply and demand of your product in the area. Sometimes, there's room for more suppliers. But don't guess. Do the research. Sometimes you will want to be in an area with lots of competition. For instance, with a restaurant, you've heard the expression "restaurant row." That's where people go when they're heading out to dinner. When people go to restaurant row, they know that if one restaurant is too busy, there will most likely be a seat in a restaurant close by. In the restaurant business, a location right next door to a similar business might be just what you need. But like I said, don't guess. Do the research.

An attractive location is also important. A run-down area of town is a bad location for any business. A dilapidated area of town sometimes symbolizes an unsafe or possibly a high crime rate area and your customers won't want to go there.

> Joe Benetti, Benetti's Italian Restaurant, mayor of Coos Bay, Oregon — The area around my business really needed fixing up, especially the boardwalk area across the street. I complained to the city and talked to my customers and they said, "Well you know, if you run for city council, you can fix it," so I did. It took eight years to get it done, but we got it done.

Purchasing your business's location has many benefits. Sometimes it's just not possible or cost-effective up front. But if it's doable for you, you should take the gamble.

Abigail Ashworth's first business, Cut and Run, was a mobile salon business where, other than working out of her home occasionally, she would go to her clients' homes to work. In her second business, she rented a retail space. Her business, Personal Touch Of Hair Design, had to relocate because the building owner was tearing down her building. Her second location for that business had the same "tenant" problems. Owning her building would have given her more control and stability.

Abigail Ashworth, Personal Touch Of Hair Design, Coos Bay, Oregon — I closed the business because I was working alone and my landlord wanted to raise my rent by 20 percent.

Real estate over any period of time goes up in value. If your business fails, you still have the property value.

Joe Benetti, Benetti's Italian Restaurant, Coos Bay, Oregon — I bought my building five years after opening and I'm glad I did. I pay myself rent instead of paying a landlord rent. In the restaurant business you really need to have control of your facility or you could find yourself in deep trouble, possibly having to relocate. Even if the business doesn't work out, the building will be worth something. Besides that, we didn't have to pay home rent to anyone; we used to live above the restaurant. We had an apartment up there and it was quite the experience. There was no kitchen in the apartment so we would go down to the restaurant to cook our meals.

Flarry Marangio, F.M. Chemical Co., Inc., Ontario, California — After fifteen years we bought a building and moved the business out of the house. We still own the building and hope the equity will help with retirement.

Approximately 52 percent of new businesses are started out of the home. Home-based businesses are a great way to start out or continually operate your business. First of all, there's no extra rent. If you can start your business out of your home, do it! For information on home-based businesses see the American Home Business Association in "other helpful Web addresses" in the back of this book.

For Sale by Owner
— Buying an Existing Business or Franchise —

Sometimes it is easier to buy an established business rather than start one from scratch. About 10 percent of new business owners have purchased an existing business. I was one of them.

When I found my business, it was not advertised for sale but it was in a perfect location. I had spent a year looking for a good location and nothing had come through for me. I saw this place; it was a dump in a perfect location. The owner obviously had failed due to neglect. I offered to buy it, he couldn't wait to sell it, and we worked out a fair deal — that was the easy part.

> Scott Farlow, Fambiz, Inc., dba Sears, North Bend, Oregon — Sometimes it can be a very hard struggle buying an existing business because of what someone

else has created. The previous owner in my business, I heard, was not well thought of in our community. Several of his customers had left but have now returned to Sears because they heard the store was under new ownership. Now they are giving it another shot and I have a chance to earn those customers back.

If you're looking into buying an existing business, find out why it is for sale. This can be a challenge of its own. Is it for sale because it is not successful? Was the seller doing it wrong? Were they doing it right? Was it a bad location, or a good location gone bad? Was the seller just bad at marketing? Is there an illness or retirement? You need to research, research, and research some more.

Abigail Ashworth, Personal Touch Of Hair Design, Coos Bay, Oregon — It was not the way to buy a business. There was never any inventory count or anything; it was just that the owner wanted to sell the business and she wanted a specific amount of money for it. So we went back and forth until we said we would give her a set amount and we wanted her to replace the water heater as part of the deal. She accepted the monetary offer but left us to deal with the water heater, and that was it.

The salon had three different kinds of flooring and four different kinds of walls. The ceiling was bare wood and above us people would walk around and

we'd have dust coming down through it. It was an old
building and it was falling off its pylons.

But the seller left all her records and introduced us to
most of her clients. She stayed and worked with me
for about two weeks.

**The myth is, you'll make up the cost of purchasing
the business in the first year.**

**The truth is, a large amount of business sellers ask
more for their business than the fair value.**

Remember, you are looking into buying their "baby." Don't
let their emotional status, or yours, deter you from making a
smart judgment.

If you purchase a successful business, it will already have a
clientele and financial records showing profits. Still, I would
always seek professional help when determining if the
business is worth the asking price. Look in your local
telephone directory for business appraisers or consultants.
Roy Metzger was a CPA in California and now resides in
Oregon. He has a degree in accounting, a Master's degree in
both business administration and financial management, and
is a member of the Accredited Institute of Business
Appraisers and the American Society of Appraisers. Roy now
specializes in business management and appraisals.

Roy Metzger, MBA, AIBA, Coos Bay, Oregon —
There are three ways to value a business: asset
approach, market approach, and income approach.

With the asset approach, Roy says you need to look at what the assets are worth in today's market. Look first at tangible items like inventory and store fixtures or office furniture. Then add value into non-tangible things like copyrights, patents, and goodwill. With the market approach, you need to look at what similar businesses sell for in your area. Finally, the income approach is the business's net income before income taxes. Remember, you're buying the cash flow of the business. Also, Roy says that some businesses are valued higher at certain times of the year.

Roy suggests avoiding using a Certified Public Accountant to appraise a business. A CPA has to use the bookkeeping to legally appraise the business, and as most of us know, books are not always accurate. By using a professional business appraiser, you'll be able to get past the bookkeeping and into the heart of the business. The cost of a professional business appraiser will depend on the size of the business, how good the financial records are, and simply the amount of work involved with the specific type of business.

After you've settled on the fair value, offer the seller no more than the fair value and include in the deal that the seller will work with you in the business for at least one month. If

the seller doesn't want to cooperate, pay attention. There may
be a reason.

Only 2 percent of business owners have purchased a franchise
business. There are benefits as well as negatives to buying a
franchise business.

> Rick Gitchen, Seattle's Best Coffee®, Chino Hills,
> California — After two years of success with Majestic
> Coffee — our first coffee house — we were looking
> for an opportunity to expand. We started looking into
> shopping center developments and talking to the
> leasing agents. The problem we were running into was
> the same problem most small businesses run into. A
> leasing agent for a new shopping center would rather
> have a big name come in and build their place than
> the local mom and pop business. So we were getting
> shut out by Starbucks at every turn and for every
> decent location that we would inquire about. To
> expand we needed some clout behind us, and the price
> of that is a franchise.
>
> At a restaurant trade show we became acquainted with
> a fellow who was representing Seattle's Best Coffee
> as a franchise opportunity. At the time, Seattle's Best
> Coffee was the number two coffee house operation in
> Seattle — Starbucks being number one. As franchises
> went, at the time, SBC was pretty reasonable. There
> was a buy-in and royalty payments of 6 percent. That

was a pretty small investment in order to get that kind of clout, and sure enough, as soon as we were able to get the franchise, opportunities started presenting themselves.

There's always a royalty payment associated with a franchise. You have to pay to get their name and expertise, but for us it was equivalent to having entry into places that we couldn't otherwise get into. It was a tremendous investment that paid off. So I guess that proves the old adage that it takes money to make money. We were very fortunate — we were profitable from day one in every store that we opened. But that's not to say that every franchise is profitable.

In addition to being able to get into better locations, a franchise is good because it gives us an opportunity to share in the corporate resourses that would otherwise be too expensive to us. The downside to a franchise is that I don't have independent choices on how to run my business in terms of the product that I'm going to sell in my store. I've lost a certain amount of my independence. But in reality, if you're in business to make money, then the only effective issue for you is the amount of profit at the end of the month. If you're in it for your personal vanity and you want to have a place that's "your place" and do everything that you want when you want to do it, go ahead and take that risk, but don't buy a franchise.

Franchises come with their own individual set of rules. Before you sign on the dotted line for a franchise, hire a legal adviser to overlook the contract. The Website for the International Franchise Association is listed under "other helpful Web addresses" in the back of this book. They can be helpful to you by answering questions about franchises.

There is another type of business that falls somewhere between independently operated and buying a franchise. Scott Farlow has that type of business. Scott owns a Sears store but is not a Sears franchise business. Scott's is considered a "dealer store."

> Scott Farlow, Fambiz, Inc., dba Sears, North Bend, Oregon — I signed a contract with Sears to sell their merchandise and I receive a commission from them for the merchandise I sell. I take care of our customers and promote Sears products, Sears credit, and Sears warranties. Under my contract I cannot sell any merchandise in my store that is not provided by Sears. But I do not pay royalties like a franchise.

I have listed a Website in the back of this book that can provide you information on this type of dealer store program through Sears.

Can't We All Just Get Along?
— The Competition —

When I purchased my ranch, like I previously stated, there were some similar businesses in the area. To make things even harder for my reopening the ranch in a competitive environment, it had a terrible reputation to overcome. The first time I walked into the local feed supply store and informed the clerk that I was the person who had purchased the ranch, she responded by saying, "Yuk, you bought that place?" I wasn't too surprised; the ranch wasn't in very good condition. After that statement, I went to work cleaning the place up and beginning the journey to repair the damage. I slowly built a better reputation for my facility by offering cleaner, safer, and better-managed stables than had existed there before I took it over. Funny thing is, that clerk became a good friend of mine and later was one of my best referrals for new customers.

Building a better business is certainly a good direction on the road to success. But other businesses shouldn't always be considered as your competition. You can work hand in hand with other companies. One of my favorite sayings is "don't burn your bridges." When I bought my business, I went out and met other ranch owners and managers in the area. I simply introduced myself and explained my intentions to renovate the ranch I had purchased. We discussed the services available at their facilities, and the services I would be able to offer. In doing this, we found that many of the services were different. So I would refer new clients to them, and they would refer new clients to me, depending on what the new clients specific needs were. Their ranch might have been more of an adult setting, and mine more a family environment. So if a new client came to me first, wanting an adult environment, I would refer them to the other ranch, and vice versa. Now this might sound like a slow way to get clients, but when trying to get a new client, you have to get their trust first. And when you get them, you'll obviously want to keep them. They have to be happy and satisfied they are getting the product they want. What we were doing was looking out for the customer as well as ourselves.

The myth is, there will be lots of customers knocking down the door to get in.

The truth is, customers never forget who they like and trust, and they'll be faithful to that.

You will never have every item a customer is looking for. So if you can't give them exactly what they need, don't substitute a less suitable product. Send them to a competitor who you know has the exact product they want. It's good to tell them to let the other company know you referred them. Keep those bridges open.

Some of your competitors might not be so willing to share information or potential clients with you. Those will probably turn out to be competitors you wouldn't want to trust anyway.

Their clients may not be able to trust them either, and may end up being your clients later. Be honest with your customers right from the start. That will be the only way to keep them for the long haul. Dishonest businesses very rarely succeed for any long period of time. You can lie your way into short-term, moneymaking business. But it won't last. If you can't go in to it honestly, don't do it.

I heard a report on the radio about a major university professor who had to fail 30 percent of his class for cheating. He caught the students with answer notes to the exam he had given. What was the class? Business etiquette. Maybe that is the reason for such a high failure rate in business.

> Jim Pioke, Ace and Bubba Treasure Hunters, Racine, Wisconsin — The very cornerstone of any successful business in the long term is honesty and dependability. You can scam people for a short period of time, but eventually that catches up to you.

I had a customer who boarded her horses with me at my ranch for two years. She taught riding lessons and even worked for me part time for a while. She started working for me because she was continually late with her boarding fees and working for me was a way she could catch up. She decided she wanted to start her own boarding ranch in the town next to mine. I was in full support of her idea and I even told her that I didn't mind if she told my existing customers about her ranch. She asked several of my customers if they would want to move their horses over to her new ranch. I had faith that my customers were happy where they were and most likely would not move. Almost all of my customers who she approached declined the offer as I expected they would. She became irritated at this reaction and began harassing my clients, continually offering huge breaks in boarding fees and to cater to their every wish. I received complaints from my clients who wanted her to stop approaching them about moving. So I asked her to leave them alone and I explained to her that what she was doing was unethical. I explained to her that in business you don't ever want to burn your bridges with your competitors. Mine was a large facility and I had many friends in the industry that could help her get started or shut her down. She ignored my request and opened her ranch with only two of my customers giving in to her harassment and following her. Within the first week, one of those customers called me and stated that they were very unhappy with the move and asked me to come and pick up their horses and bring them back to my facility. Just over a month into her new boarding business, I received a call from my hay dealer wanting to know if her credit was good and whether or not she would pay the bill on time. I told him she had been late on her boarding bill with me and I did not feel she was reliable. Without a good reference to buy feed, she was forced to close her ranch.

Some other business owners can be sharks and eat you alive. Staying ahead of the game will keep you in business. Honesty is the only road to long-term success. Customers won't tolerate liars and cheats. Your competition will most likely bury you at the first sign of dishonesty — as they probably should.

If you play golf, picture this: the business owner takes his client out for a round of golf. They're on a par five hole — "par" is if they get the ball in the hole in only five shots. The business owner doesn't like his first tee shot, so he says he'll take a mulligan. A mulligan is a free shot, and to many is not considered ethical. The group heads out for their next shots, and the business owner hits his second (really third) shot out of bounds. He drops another ball to hit, and of course, that one's gone too. (Shot number six, number seven? I've lost count.) The next thing the client hears is, "just put me down for a bogie six." Now if this business owner were this dishonest in a game, would you trust them in business? Good thing he doesn't play golf with his competitors!

"What Will It Take?"

Street Smarts
— Education and Planning —

Who will make a good entrepreneur? There are many scientific theories floating around out there: the genetic theory, your parents' child-rearing techniques, or the birth order in your family (being the first born might make you more successful). By the way, I was the sixth child born in my family, so I can't agree with that last theory. Being the youngest in a large family, I had to fight for everything. I had to negotiate everything I wanted from my parents, and by that time my siblings had already tried nearly every angle with them. Having to fight for what you want is good preparation for self-employment.

Anyone can be an entrepreneur. Anything could have developed in your life to create an entrepreneurial type of personality. Leadership and what drives you is learned by your lifes experiences. Most entrepreneurs don't have formal training or education but have a passion and a desire to succeed.

The founder of Dell Computers was a college dropout. Starting out of his garage, he managed to excel above all of the world's top computer manufacturers. One in three computers sold today is a Dell.

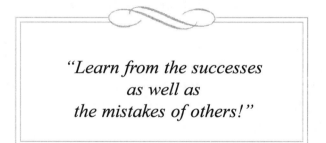

*"Learn from the successes
as well as
the mistakes of others!"*

The person who has the best chance of having a successful business does not necessarily need to have a Master's degree. According to a 1992 United States Census Bureau report, only 5.3 percent of business owners have a Master's degree or higher education. 9.4 percent had less than a high school education — some only up to the eighth grade. The largest percentage (26 percent) had some college, and 24 percent did complete college. Oddly enough, only 17 percent had any business education. I never finished the tenth grade, but I did go back for my equivalency diploma. Let me add, education is priceless! While I was successful in the end, if I had more education early on I would have made fewer mistakes and saved myself a bunch of headaches. The first time you make a mistake, it is a learning experience. The second time you make the same mistake, it's stupidity — get educated. Read good books relating to your type of business and get the education you need to avoid those mistakes the first time.

The myth is, you are highly educated and you have a Master's degree — you can't lose.

The truth is, even if you have education and experience in the field you have chosen, you can never know it all.

Abigail Ashworth, Personal Touch Of Hair Design, Coos Bay, Oregon — I taught hair design for ten years. I taught while I was operating my first business.

> Dan Abel, AD Construction and Remodel, LLC, Coos
> Bay, Oregon — It isn't just a financial investment,
> it's an investment in knowledge. Even your mistakes
> can be a learning tool and sometimes they can be a
> better learning tool than success, even if they hurt.

Robert Stevenson is the author of the book *How to Soar Like an Eagle in a World Full of Turkeys*. He has owned and operated his own successful companies. He is a public speaker on the subject of customer service and conducts seminars for large corporations and small businesses across the United States. For more information on Robert Stevenson visit www.robertstevenson.org.

> Robert Stevenson, business owner and author —
> Seeking excellence is a continuous journey where we
> should learn from the past, deal with the present,
> prepare for the future, and appreciate it all.

Preparing for the future means planning. Of all the interviews I did with small business owners, almost all of them had struggles with success due to lack of planning.

> Jim Pionke, Ace and Bubba Treasure Hunters, Racine,
> Wisconsin — I'm embarrassed to say this because I
> used to teach Small Business Management classes,
> but I went in without a plan.

Joe Benetti, Benetti's Italian Restaurant, Coos Bay, Oregon — The first day we opened, customers would come up to the counter and order. I just took their order on scratch paper. I didn't have an order ticket to tear off and give them. So we would wander around asking the customers what they had ordered. We also didn't have a wheel, the thing you clip the order slip onto for the cook. So we laid out the orders for the cook and the fan would blow them everywhere. So the next day I had a wheel and I had tickets you could tear in two. So that's how we started and we learned as we went along. Knowing what I know today, I was very lucky and fortunate to make it; normally, that's just not going to be the case. When you open a restaurant, or any business, make sure you are overstaffed and over prepared because your first impression will be a long lasting one.

A business plan is crucial to success. Businesses owners going in without a plan generally fail, or at a minimum, suffer unnecessary delays in their success.

Scott Farlow, Fambiz, Inc., dba Sears, North Bend, Oregon — It is very important to do at least a three-year business plan and definitely seek legal council before signing any contracts or leases.

Some people feel they "have it all in their head" and they know where to go with it. I say those people have something else in their head — a fantasy. Putting a plan down on paper makes it real.

Pete and Leslie Lawson own and operate two golf courses in Arizona. The golf courses were their third attempt at self-employment and their first success. Turquoise Valley Golf Course has been listed as one of Arizona's top golf courses. In 2004, it was chosen AETNA Insurance Small Business of the Year.

> Pete Lawson, Turquoise Valley Golf and RV Resort, Naco, Arizona — If I were to do it over again, I would probably sit down on the computer and hammer it out for six months before I would spend one dollar. You must have the smarts and the research to prove it can happen. If you don't have that, then work for somebody else.

The myth is, whatever you didn't plan for will somehow work itself out.

The truth is, lack of planning is the biggest reason for business failure.

If you're going to invest all that it takes emotionally and financially into starting your own company, take every precaution to make it a success. If not, why bother at all? If you're heading to the bank for a small business loan, a business plan will most likely be required with your application. If you need a business plan to apply for a loan, go to a bookstore or your local library and pick up a book specifically on writing a business plan. I have listed my favorite reference book for writing a business plan under the "recommended reading" section in the back of this book.

*"People don't plan
to fail, but some
fail to plan!"*

A business plan is simple. Follow some of these guidelines for your plan.

- List what you want and where you want to be in one year, three years, and five years.
- Research the industry you want to pursue.
- List what the competition is.
- Make a financial list of expenditures and start-up costs (these can kill you). See worksheets, pages 88 and 89.
- List your household income until you can show a profit.
- List your advertising strategies and costs.

Part of a good business plan is to physically go out and inspect what other similar businesses are doing to be successful, or what they're not doing. Learn by watching and researching your type of business.

Rick and Dan Gitchen presently own seven Seattle's Best Coffee franchise stores, five in Las Vegas, Nevada, one store in Irvine, California, and one store in Chino Hills, California with a total gross income of over three million dollars a year. How do you think they were so successful? Take a look at the research they did.

> Rick Gitchen, Seattle's Best Coffee®, Chino Hills, California — Our first three months we researched into the coffee house business. We would go to coffee house after coffee house in several cities and visit

every chain like Starbucks, or the mom and pop coffee houses — anywhere coffee was sold. We would sit in them hours and hours and watch everything they were doing. We had these little counters to count the number of drinks sold. We would try to calculate how much business they were doing in the course of an hour based on what most people were ordering, the average drink, etc. Through the course of our research — which ended up totaling about nine months — we were able to get a real good handle on the business before we opened it. Our hands-on research allowed us to see how other places were operating, how many people they were having work at certain times, and what the overhead would be. Through that we figured out it could be a profitable business if it was done correctly. We opened our first coffee house, Majestic Coffee, in 1994. We now have seven coffee houses with a gross annual income of over three million dollars.

James and Sandy Flanagan have been operating an equestrian center in Chino, California for over three years.

Sandra Flanagan, Prado Equestrian Center, LLC, Chino, California — The one thing you need to do more than anything, and the one thing most businesses don't sit down and do is plan. Customers expect you to raise the bar no matter what kind of business you're in and you can't do that without planning.

You also need to plan for the licenses, permits, and zoning requirements for your new business. There might also be additional taxes due on any specific business. It will be up to you alone to research what those might be. Some of them might be:

- Zoning requirements
- Local permits
- Local business licenses
- State and federal licenses
- Resale permits
- Sales taxes
- State and federal taxes
- Use tax
- IRS requirements
- Federal trade commission rules
- And if you plan to hire help, there will certainly be state and federal regulations to follow.

Every business will require some type of permit or license to operate. You will need to contact your local county and city government offices to find out which apply to your specific business.

If you sell products or services on which your state charges sales tax, you must apply for a seller's permit (also called a resale permit). You will be responsible for collecting sales tax and turning it over to the state annually, quarterly, or monthly depending on your volume of business.

You might need to research trademarks, copyrights, and patents.

If you offer a unique product or service, and especially if you serve a widespread clientele, registering your trademark may be advisable. Helpful Web addresses to help you research trademarks, copyrights, patents, and many of the permits and licenses that may be required are listed under "helpful federal government Web addresses" in the back of this book.

In most states, if you are doing business under any other than your own name (that is, not just "John Doe," but "John Does Mortuary"), you will need to file a fictitious name statement, also known as a dba ("doing business as"). Without a dba, you probably will not be able to obtain a city business license or open a bank account in the name of your business. To file a dba you will need to obtain and file a form with the appropriate government agency and then publish your fictitious name in a newspaper that carries fictitious name statements.

You also might want to look into protecting your personal assets by setting up a full corporation or an LLC — a limited liability corporation. A good attorney can help you with this process. It is worth the investment and absolutely a must if you are starting a high-risk business. A high-risk business would be any business that someone could get hurt. Most businesses run the risk of a customer getting injured. Even at a retail store if a customer slips on your freshly waxed floor, you could be held liable for a lifetime of someone's pain and suffering. Protect yourself.

Will That Be All?
— Customer Service —

Prior to owning my own business, I worked in the customer service industry for nine years. It was there I learned the importance of good customer service. The lessons I learned definitely contributed to my success with my own company.

Customer service, or really "service the customer," is the number one key to success. Are you good at "ass kissing?" You'll need it for this part of your business.

> Pete Lawson, Turquoise Valley Golf and RV Resort, Naco, Arizona — Repeat business is the ground on which you build. Kissing the public's butt is absolutely the number one most important thing to your success.

I love to hear people say things like, "I hate kissing up to my boss." If you're one of those people, quit this self-employment idea right now. Out of all businesses, 52 percent will sell their product directly to the public. When you get into a customer service business, every customer you have will be like another boss for you. If you have one hundred customers, you have one hundred bosses. Even if you only have one customer, you always have to keep your boss happy, right? Now you'll have to keep your customer happy the same way. You'll have to do the job right, and, like your job now, to get any promotions, or in this case, more business, you'll have to go above and beyond.

Of customers leaving a business, 15 percent of them stated they left because they didn't like the quality, 15 percent because of the price, and 70 percent said they didn't like the "human side" of the business. The human side is clearly the biggest part of customer service. 96 percent of your customers with problems will never tell you they have a problem. They will simply take their business to the competition.

> Robert Stevenson, business owner and author — If you don't know what it takes to make your customer say "WOW," you probably won't be around long.

Let me give you an example of customer service. Sears and JC Penny are two of the more popular department stores that have been in business for many years. When a new department store named Nordstrom opened, the chance of Nordstrom's success was minimal. So Nordstrom adopted a plan to provide the best customer service possible, above and beyond what the other stores gave their customers. Their plan was to gain the trust of their customers through unconditional service.

Here's a story Nordstrom uses to teach future sales clerks about the stores commitment to customer service. An elderly woman drives in to a Nordstrom with a flat tire. The woman wanted to exchange the tire. The Nordstrom clerk informed her that Nordstrom did not sell tires. The woman argued she was certain she had purchased the tire at Nordstrom. Now even though Nordstrom did not sell tires, the clerk took the tire to a local tire shop that sold that brand of tire and purchased a new one. He then went back to his store and installed the new tire on the woman's car. That *is* customer service.

Nordstrom has a policy of accepting almost any returns, no questions asked. Nordstrom sales far surpassed the sales of Sears and JC Penny within their first few years of business. I believe this can be credited to their customer service policy.

> Joe Benetti, Benetti's Italian Restaurant, Coos Bay, Oregon — The customer is always right. Even when they're wrong, they're right. Period.

In my business I tried to follow a similar policy. If one of my customers called me at two a.m. because they thought their horse was ill or injured, I would get out of bed and go down to the stables. It may have turned out to be something minor, but I would never show any irritation for being dragged out of bed. Instead, I would always tell that customer to call me anytime and I would be there again. When something is important to your customer, it should be just as important to you.

> Maria Aarvig, Creason and Aarvig, LLP, attorney, Riverside, California — People have to be trusting enough to send you business and that isn't because you got good grades in college. It's all about character and personality.

With prospective customers, you'll need to be very upfront with them right from the start. You'll need to let them know just what service or product you will provide them with. For instance, when a potential customer came to me, I would clearly inform them of the extent of my service. I would be providing their horse with daily feed, a certain amount of feed, and a certain type of feed. I would inform them about how often the stall and water system would be cleaned, the facility available to them, and other services available for additional fees. I would be very clear about what was not included in my basic fee. I would always add things at last minute to please the customer, and, most importantly, I would always follow through. You may or may not find the need to have a contract for service provided. But regardless of contracts and your services provided, it is very important to go above and beyond in many circumstances. It will only gain additional loyalty from your customers if you do more for them than originally agreed upon in a written or verbal contract.

What brings you back to a good restaurant? Obviously, the food is a good answer. But even if the food is great, if every time you go there you have to wait an hour for your meal, do you think twice before choosing that restaurant again? When you take your car to a carwash and they do a poor job of cleaning it, do you hesitate to take it to that carwash next time? Unless they are lucky enough to have the only restaurant or carwash in town, they are destined for failure. Even if those businesses did a so-so job of customer service, they probably are barely surviving in business. If your business plan ever includes growth or expansion of any kind, you will need to be better than your average competitor.

"If you have no customers,
you won't sell your product.
If you don't sell your product,
you have no business."

Try the following quiz to measure your ability and willingness to provide great customer service.

Yes   No

[   ]   [   ] Sales are down in your business — a customer has returned an item without good reason. Do you immediately take the item back and refund the customer's money?

[   ]   [   ] You're having a really bad day. Your wife is mad at you, you had an argument with your teenager, and your dog ate your wallet. Can you greet your next customer with a genuine, helpful smile?

[   ]   [   ] You're an electrician, and your customer has lost all power in their home unrelated to their utility company supply. You have tickets to a baseball game. Do you pass on the ball game to help your customer?

[   ]   [   ] You are a general contractor. You are building a new home for a client. Your client's previous home has already sold and they are living in a hotel until their new home is completed. Bad weather has delayed construction. Do you work through the weekends to finish the home more quickly?

[   ]   [   ] You've been running business related errands all day. You arrive at your office late Friday afternoon to find you have thirty new phone messages. The last message

is from your spouse. He or she wants to meet you for an early dinner. Do you pass on the dinner invitation and stay late to return those twenty-nine other calls?

[   ]   [   ] A customer comes to you with a special order for an item you normally don't carry. You can get the item, but it's a hassle. Do you make the extra effort to get the item for the customer rather than sending them elsewhere?

If you answered yes to all of the questions above, you have what it takes to provide exceptional customer service. Even if you hesitated on your yes answers, you have shown a willingness to satisfy your customers. Nobody wants to give up ball game seats or pass on a romantic dinner, but sometimes it's necessary to keep a good customer. As I've said before, good customers are hard to get. When you get them, you must battle to keep them.

> Robert Stevenson, business owner and author — The day we forget we are in business because of the customer, is the day we start going out of business.

The myth is, everyone will want your product and customer service won't apply in your type of business.

The truth is, customer service always applies to

your business. Great customer service above and beyond is your best bet for gaining customer loyalty.

Great customer service is your best chance to have a growing and prosperous business. I'm sure you're not considering self-employment as just a way to barely get by. So write out your plans for providing top quality customer service to your customers, and stick to your plan.

> Flarry Marangio, F.M. Chemical Co. Inc., Ontario, California — The relationship you have with your customer is your bread and butter.

Of course, at times you will have customers who seem impossible to please. If you have given them 110 percent, and still they're not satisfied, they will most likely move on to a competitor. But in my own experience, I have found they generally come back and are more reasonable with their expectations the second time around. The grass isn't always greener on the other side of the fence. Then there will be those customers who are labeled "impossible-to-deal-with" — every business will have them. When those customers leave you, be glad and let them go on. You will have enough headaches with your business without adding to it. Those impossible to deal with customers end up taking time away from your good customers. The bad news is that one happy customer will tell four other people good things about your business, and that unhappy customer will tell *twenty* other people bad things. So with those statistics, try your best to satisfy everyone. It is possible for a bad customer to leave on good terms. Try your best to be friendly with them when they are moving on. Maybe even suggest a competitor to them. I wouldn't necessarily suggest a competitor you have good relationships with, but you might even call ahead to your competitor and let them know this person was unhappy with your service and warn them of the situation. They may do the same for you some day.

Marketing your product or service can be your biggest challenge, but remember: no sales, no money! Wasting time, effort, and especially money on poor avenues of marketing can really slow down your success. The hardest part of my business was trying to reach my potential customers through advertising. Many of the choices I made were costly and didn't produce new sales. I strongly suggest you research your market and learn how to reach those customers. Marketing is an art form, so go take an art class.

Through advertising, the average cost of getting one new customer at your door is over one hundred dollars. So when you get someone in the door, you need to work very hard at customer service to keep them. That will generally start with a phone call. If you want to know how good your company is, call it!

Abigail Ashworth, Personal Touch Of Hair Design, Coos Bay, Oregon — It starts right over the phone. If you don't have that smile in your voice when you answer the phone, they're either not going to make that appointment or they're not going to call back.

"A satisfied customer is a return customer. Return customers make a business successful!"

In any business, answering the phone is extremely important. Let's say, for instance, you come home to find a plumbing line has burst in your house. There is water everywhere, and unless you are talented at fixing broken pipes, you will grab the phone book and search for a plumber. If you call a plumber listed, and nobody answers the phone, wouldn't you just go down the phone book listings until somebody answers? Those plumbers who didn't answer the phone lost your business. The one who answered your call has the opportunity to gain a new customer. But that's not all there is to it. People get their first impression of you over the phone. Here's where that customer service really comes in. Let's say you're the plumber who answered the phone. If you come off sounding like you're just too busy or distracted, you are sending a signal to the customer that you don't really care about their problem. If you are helpful and reassuring, you will always have made a good impression. Follow that up with above and beyond service, and you will have a faithful new customer. In most cases, it pays you back to have someone attending to the incoming phone calls.

The business I purchased had the same phone number for eleven years, and I was able to keep the number. But the business was so run down, that I sat at the phone for two days before it finally rang, and even then, sadly, it was a wrong number. A day later, it rang again, and that call was from an old friend of my business's previous owner. So when that phone finally rang for me and my new business, you can bet I put on a good customer service attitude! But whether it's that one call, or hundreds of calls, you better be prepared to answer with your best customer service attitude.

"You never get a second chance to make a good impression."

With online businesses, customer service comes into the game at a minimum. It's always easier and less time consuming when you don't have to talk face to face with your customers. If you're uncomfortable dealing directly with people, this type of business might be just right for you.

> Roberta Abel, Giftabel.com, Coos Bay, Oregon — For the most part, I don't even have to talk to my customers and that was my whole goal — I knew I wouldn't have the time. Direct customer service doesn't apply too often with an online business. My customers only care that their orders are filled quickly and shipped properly. Sometimes if there's a problem with an order, I will e-mail my customer, and once in a while, I do still feel the need to call them.

For the Love of Money
— Cash Investment —

People seem to always underestimate their start-up costs and monthly expenses for a new business. They especially underestimate their living expenses while the business is not yet showing profits. Two of the business owners I interviewed were fortunate enough to be able to live in the same commercial building they did business in, but that's not likely going to be an option for you unless you operate your business out of your home. Even then, I'm sure that mortgage payments or rent are not your only personal expenses.

There will be a significant cash investment required to purchase a business or start a new one. I'm not speaking of the purchase price alone. Experts suggest you have not only the cash to purchase or start the business, but also enough savings in addition to that to support your household for one year or more. According to a 2002 United States Census Bureau study, if you can survive the first year in business, your chances for success increase. The same study showed that 39 percent of business owners said their lack of initial capital had an impact on their profits. Remember, no profits, no business! So you need a significant amount of money to be able to stay in the game.

Now let's talk about business finance. Reports show that 27 percent of business owners borrowed the money they needed to start their business. I don't recommend borrowing money to start up if you can avoid doing so. 36.5 percent of owners used their savings to start their business. It is always better to save the money you need up front. A total of 69 percent of new businesses were started or acquired without the need to borrow any money at all.

> Pete Lawson, Turquoise Valley Golf and RV Resort, Naco, Arizona — It was a huge cash investment with a lot of surprises. Potential business owners need to

have a plan, a plan they can follow through with. If
you don't have additional resources, or a good solid
financial plan, you're going to be in trouble. We didn't
take a loan, and that is probably the only reason we
were successful.

**The myth is, your great business idea can't fail, and
you will be making profits the first month.**

**The truth is, most businesses will not show any
profit for at least the first year, and the average
time is around three years.**

Just over one third of new business owners needed less than
$5,000 to start or acquire their business. Amazingly enough,
25 percent of new business' were started with no money up
front.

Dan Abel, AD Construction and Remodeling, LLC,
Coos Bay, Oregon — You kind of have to know what
you're capable of doing. When I first started the
business I was doing small jobs, so all I needed was a
skill saw, a hammer, and a few other tools.

Rick Gitchen, Seattle's Best Coffee®, Chino Hills,
California — When starting out, you want to make
absolutely sure you are not jeopardizing the welfare
of your family to take this risk. Everyone I know in
my business that failed, did so because they weren't

financially secure enough, they weren't capitalized enough to enter into their business, and the debt ended up overwhelming them. Even if you're doing an SBA (small business administration) loan, typically they want that loan secured to your house and you run the risk of losing your home.

If you have a business idea, you need to keep it in proportion to the amount of money you have to pursue it. Instead of building a $400,000 franchise store, you might need to look at buying a $15,000 coffee cart that you can drive around to local events. There's always a way to work out your idea without exceeding your means.

When I bought my business, we had savings to invest and we borrowed only 20 percent of the purchase price. My advantage was that my spouse had another career and was the greater financial provider, and my regular job was only supplemental income for the family. I also worked evenings, leaving my days free. I may not have succeeded under other circumstances. My business showed a loss for the first year, and only broke even the second year. My tax accountant was disappointed in me because I had purchased a horse boarding business. He said they never make money. It took me three years to prove him wrong. It was the third year in business that I found myself single again and without that financial provider — my husband — and I had inherited all the bills. I was left with no choice but to force more income out of the business and that meant more hours and more work. But I showed my first profit in year three and was able to pay all of those bills.

In the year that I bought my losing business, the estimated odds of succeeding past the first year in a new business were only 5 percent. Out of that 5 percent, the estimated odds of succeeding another five years were only 10 percent. If you need a calculator to figure out that the odds weren't good, you had better add some math courses to my suggested education. I'm certain the reason for such a low success rate at that time was a weak economy, but also insufficient startup fund availability for the new business owner. We all would like to think that we are smart enough, or experienced enough to succeed on a less than suggested amount of investment, but we are not. On top of that, at some time during the operation of more recent businesses surveyed, 74 percent of businesses needed to borrow additional capital just to keep going.

I knew of one woman who had signed up for seventeen credit cards on the same day so she could get enough cash advance money to start her business. In my opinion, this woman didn't have the common sense of sand. It's hard to believe that people like that would expect to succeed. She didn't.

Rick Gitchen, Seattle's Best Coffee®, Chino Hills, California — Using credit cards is the most risky form of financing that there is, and you have to have some really serious confidence. If it's possible to get another type of loan, that would be preferable. Credit cards should be the last resort because it's just so dangerous if you don't service the debt.

Let me tell you right now why I chose this topic to write a book about. I have witnessed so many sad stories of failure. Families torn apart or financially devastated due to lack of planning for their business venture. People were taking equity loans on their homes for startup funds, and then losing their homes to the bank. Your equity in your home should never be touched. That might someday be your retirement, and people running their own business very rarely see retirement. By writing this book, I am hoping you can gain the foresight to plan properly and not rush things for a greater chance of success in the long haul.

Use the worksheet below to figure what the majority of your start-up costs will be.

**Start Up Expenditures
Total Cost**

Inventory
(don't sell yourself short) .... $_____

Business location initial down payment,
deposits, or rents .... $ _____

Utility and security deposits .... $ _____

Permits, licenses, and inspection fees .... $ _____

Insurance .... $ _____

Advertising (wow, this can be big!) .... $ _____

Store front signage if needed .... $ _____

Equipment purchase or rental .... $ _____

Stationary, business cards, postage .... $ _____

Other .... $ _____

Total start-up expenditures .... $ _____

In addition to start-up costs, you must plan for the monthly expenses that come with the operation of your new business. Use the worksheet below to figure what the majority of your monthly expenses will be.

Monthly Expenditures
Total Cost

Monthly location payment or rent .... $ _____

Utility bills (water, electric, gas, propane) $ _____

Phone expenses — hard line, cellular, fax,
Internet service, long distance .... $ _____

Insurance .... $ _____

Equipment payments or rental fees .... $ _____

Monthly advertising .... $ _____

Employees .... $ _____

Office supplies .... $ _____

Other .... $ _____

Total monthly expenditures .... $ _____

Don't forget to include household expenses. Since household expenses change monthly, the most simplistic means I have found for estimating your monthly expenses is to search your checkbook log for the past year. List all expenses related to your everyday life. Don't forget car payments, insurance, deductibles, and even the kid's soccer uniform (uncommon expenses). Total it up and divide by twelve. That will give you a more realistic total rather than just food, gas, rent, etc.

Don't Feed The Pig — Advertising Hogs —

Start-up and operating expenses can be eaten up fast by unnecessary costs in business. When you are starting out, be aware of every dime spent. Properly advertising your new business is crucial to its success, but don't feed the pig. Advertisers always try to convince you that their methods will work the best. They will fight for your entire advertising budget, and then bring you no customers. The truth is, there is no one perfect way to advertise your business. You should spread your dollars in to several methods of advertising. Testing the water of several different methods will show you what works best for your business. Don't sign on to any high dollar or long term contracts until the advertising method has consistently proven itself over a long period of time.

The phone book is one of the best forms of advertising, and you'll likely want to place your business in it. But when you call to do that, they will try to sell you more — it's their job. It's easy to start the call with a thirty-dollar-a-month ad, and hang up with a commitment to a three-hundred-dollar-a-month bill, that may not bring you any more customers.

You will often find one advertising method that works very well for your type of business. When one form of advertising that has worked for a while stops working, try another. It's a continually changing industry that you must keep researching and testing.

There will be other pigs as you start your business. Equipment rentals, security systems, even port-a-potties can eat up your monthly income. When you are signing on to long-term contracts, shop around. Better yet, try not to sign on to long-term contracts. You don't know what your businesses needs will be in one, three, or five years. Many companies will offer you the same product, but for less. Don't be in a hurry.

Buy quality. Having to replace expensive equipment in a short term costs you money. You don't want your business to shut down because you bought a cheap refrigerator system for your restaurant or a telephone answering machine that rarely works. Look for good deals on good products.

New Clothes
— Changing With the Times —

Some businesses start out well and sometime later start falling apart. You have to keep up with the times. If not, someone else will and you'll be left behind wondering what happened to your booming business. Some reasons for your decline in business could be new technology, other new businesses, or just lack of new ideas and products.

> Abigail Ashworth, Personal Touch Of Hair Design, Blackwell's Salon, Coos Bay, Oregon — After a while, you can see the ones that don't change with the times. Their clientele is slowing down, they're getting older, they're not getting new clientele, and they're not able to retain new clientele. So their income starts going down and it starts hurting and they themselves become bitter. Some of them just don't care. They like doing the hair of the same little old ladies, doing the same thing the same way all the time. But those little old ladies don't stay around forever, if you know what I mean. You always have to do something to bring in new clientele and to retain new clientele when you get them.

Of the Fortune 500 companies listed in 1970, 74 percent are off the list, since 1980 46 percent are off.

The myth is, Donald Trump couldn't have filed bankruptcy, he's too wealthy.

The truth is, he did. Just because your company might make it big, that doesn't mean you'll be able to stay at the top.

Staying at the top requires constant changes and flexibility. Montgomery Ward department stores were in business for eighty-nine years with 85,000 employees, 9.3 billion dollars in revenue, and operated in 84 countries. Do you see any Montgomery Wards around? Montgomery Ward didn't change with the times.

"People are divided into three categories:
those who make it happen,
those who watch it happen,
and the rest, who wonder,
what the hell happened!"

> Robert Stevenson, author and business owner —
> Success is never final. It's not the big that eat the
> small, it's the fast that eat the slow.

You have to reinvest in your company to grow and you have to grow to keep up with other successful companies. In 1977, Dreyer's Grand ice cream had thirty-four flavors of ice cream. In 2004 they had two hundred and fifty flavors. Starbucks Coffee now has 19,000 ways to serve coffee. Do you think these companies miss opportunities for growth?

The key to long-term success is to grow and expand from within. A solid business is like a spider: there is a body that represents your main line of business, the core, the place you started. Then, as with any successful business, there are the legs, expanding out, touching new areas. In my business I boarded horses, which was my core. I could barely have made a living wage if I had not grown legs. I added products and services one by one until I had several small businesses operating out of that horse boarding business. If you open a gas station, you can add mechanical services, snack shop, or a car wash. If you sell furniture, add flooring or accessories. There's never a limit to expansion and growth.

> Roberta Abel, Giftabel.com, Coos Bay, Oregon —
> With online sales, if there's one item that everybody
> seems to be buying, there will be a lot of sites out
> there to buy it. You have to diversify to stay in the
> game. You have to always have something different
> and that's really difficult to do.

*"Business is like water skiing:
it's a challenge to get up out of the water,
and a whole different challenge
to stay up and ski."*

4

"When Disaster Strikes"

A new business owner asked the city what was needed to open a business. "I was told I only needed two things: a business license and a sales tax license. I obtained the licenses and opened a downtown store. I advertised my grand opening specials, brand name nail polish for twenty-five cents and a package of pasta for twenty-five cents.

On opening day I got cited by city licensing for not having a license to sell paint (nail polish), by grocery licensing for not having a day-old variance, and by the fire marshal for not having $900 in fire extinguishers placed in the building. The same day, the city returned to inspect the service elevator in the building, which hadn't run for over fifty years. They charged me almost $300. There were business activity taxes, interim business taxes, and inventory taxes. When I hired someone to help with the store, I got a huge pile of paperwork from the unemployment office.

I closed my business. One week later I was cited for failure to get a going-out-of-business license. Next thing I saw was the city mayor on television saying, 'We have to seek new ways of attracting new businesses to our downtown area.' "

"No matter how much you plan for things that can go wrong, you will always have forgotten something."

Just My Luck!
— Bad Luck —

Sometimes you just can't control your situation. When I had my ranch, if it rained or was too hot outside, my hourly horse rental business had to shut down for the day. Sometimes the bad weather would last for weeks at a time. The weather situation would have complete control over my monthly income.

You might also find yourself having to deal with unexpected loss of income in your business. It's hard to save a dime when you're starting out in business, but you have to set something aside to get you through the tough, unexpected financial losses. Loss of monthly income can happen due to many causes, a weak economy, or like in my business, bad weather.

Roberta Abel, Giftabel.com, Coos Bay, Oregon — When I started out, it seemed like everybody wanted to buy my gift items. At the gift shows, people would come at me with cash wanting to get one of my garden pots. Then 9/11 happened and that whole next year wasn't good. There was a different feeling in the economy during that time.

Pete Lawson, Turquoise Valley Golf and RV, Naco, Arizona — I have a beef jerky business that was doing really well at one time, and I wanted to expand. Unfortunately, when mad cow disease came about, people just quit buying any kind of beef. Now it's just barely staying active as a business.

We're Pals, Right?
— Partnerships —

I took on a partner in my business at one point to expand. He had the money to invest and wanted to be a silent partner. Soon after our partnership began, he asked me to give his son a job. His son had some experience in my type of business, so I hired him. The young man was a pretty good worker but never showed up on time and skipped days without a call. It put a tremendous strain on my other employees. My partner made lots of excuses as to why his son couldn't be there. My partner also expected his son to be paid for the time he was absent. When I refused, my partner started showing up in the place of his son. This partner of mine had absolutely no experience in this business and quickly became a thorn in my side. He began to make business decisions that directly affected my business in a way that did not make me happy. It cost me many headaches and a financial fortune to dissolve the partnership.

I'm sure you can understand why I personally don't recommend partnerships. I realize there are many that do work out extremely well. But unless the partners have completely different purposes in the business, they will generally clash.

You can only think and speak for yourself, you cannot for someone else. You can't assume what someone else is thinking, so you can never speak for your partner. Therefore, there will be differences in your decision-making as a partnership.

The myth is, your partner is your best friend, so you're likely to work well together.

The truth is, there can only be one "head."

I have personally known of only two partnerships, without being family or spousal-related, that have worked out. One was in a law firm where each of the partners practiced a specific type of law. They also practiced at different locations. So there was only one *head* at each location, and only one *head* in each type of law they practiced. The other partnership was between Jim Dalhover and Lee Wright of Commonwealth Upholstery in Fullerton, California. They've been in business over forty years. It is amazing that this partnership and the business itself have survived. The two men who owned and operated the shop were childhood friends. They opened the shop together and each had a separate job in their business. One did the sewing, the other did the fitting and paperwork. Although Lee passed away during the writing of this book, his interview quotes remain in print. Jim is in his seventies now and still operating the business.

> Lee Wright, Commonwealth Upholstery, Fullerton, California — We met in the second grade and have been friends ever since. The key to our success is trust.

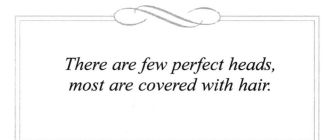

There are few perfect heads, most are covered with hair.

I would like to give you more positive feedback from business owners regarding non-family related partnerships, but unfortunately there weren't any others. Of all the small business owners I interviewed, all but two were negative about their partnership experiences. Even one of the two who had a successful partnership did not recommend it. For the most part, partnerships do not work well.

Joe Benetti, Benetti's Italian Restaurant, Coos Bay, Oregon — I've been in a partnership and I don't recommend them. If everything is going great with the business, there's not a problem. But when things get difficult and there is a problem, everyone has their own interpretation of how to solve it. You are always going to have a problem somewhere down the road.

Maria Aarvig, Creason and Aarvig, LLP, attorney, Riverside, California — I think it's really unusual for partnerships to work out very well. Coming from a lawyer's perspective, I've started a lot of partnerships, and I'd say 60 percent of them do fall apart. Partnership dissolution is like a divorce — it's really ugly. The worst situation for me, as a lawyer, is when I have friends come to me after they've developed a business, without having a business plan, without having a partnership agreement, and without having an understanding upfront about how they're going to deal with the business. Now it's falling apart and there's nothing in writing.

> If you're going to start a business with a partner, do it professionally. Get an attorney who does not represent either side. It's going to cost you about $1,500 but it's *so* worth it.

Try to avoid going into business with a partner. It's even hard to write a partnership contract that will *fully* protect you and your business should the partnership fail.

A silent partner, one who is truly silent, will sometimes work out. But when people invest their money, they usually want to see where it is going and where it is coming in. They will eventually want some involvement, which can cause conflict between partners.

The business that Flarry and Joan Marangio started in 1962 went from $100-a-month income to a six-million-dollar-a-year business. The business saw a disastrous 1.6 million dollar loss and its demise just one year after they took on three partners.

> Joan Marangio, F.M. Chemical Co., Inc., Upland, California — Being a boss is not easy. Being a boss and an owner isn't easy either. But being an owner and having another owner tell you what to do, is even more difficult. Don't take partners unless you're married to them, and even that may not be a good idea.

A strong marital or family relationship makes for a better partnership because there is an existing bond deeper than any contract. You will never hear me recommend non-family-member partnerships in this book. Some work out, but for the most part, they don't. But I would recommend spousal or family partnerships.

> Rick Gitchen, Seattle's Best Coffee®, Chino Hills, California — My brother Dan and I work really well together. When we started out, each of us had our areas that we were more interested in and had more expertise in. He had a really strong marketing background and a lot of creativity in that area. My background was more in operations, so I could run the store and he could run the relationships. It's kind of like a marriage in the sense that you are a 50 percent owner of 100 percent of the business.

With these partnerships there is a shared interest and a bond that keeps compromise alive so neither person will feel left out.

> Jim Pionke, Ace and Bubba Treasure Hunters, Racine, Wisconsin — People have different expectations of what success is and what good work habits are. If you don't have a marriage, not just a partnership, my experience is that it ultimately won't be a long-lasting relationship.

I.O.U.
— Bad Debts —

Earning money in business is one thing, trying to collect it is sometimes another story. In my business I had to process a lot of checks. I would have about one percent of them returned from the bank stamped "insufficient funds." I would eventually collect on most, but, some I never did. That might not sound like much to you, but when you receive over a hundred checks a month; you have to deal with it every month. It won't matter who that customer is, what they look like, or if they've written you good checks in the past. I had one customer who was a city council member for a major city in California. She wrote me a check that was for a fundraiser for the 9/11 tragedy. She had bought some donated merchandise at a silent auction we were having for the fundraiser. She took the donated merchandise and left. Out of all the people there that day that I knew, she probably would have been the last person I would have suspected to write a bad check. Her check bounced and was never collected on.

My customers had loads of excuses for their checks bouncing, and some were legitimate. But let me tell you one excuse I heard more than once. The customer told me they had checked their balance through the ATM machine the day they wrote the check and the money was in the bank. When I asked them about possibly having other checks or transactions that hadn't yet cleared the bank when they checked the balance, they looked dumbfounded.

The myth is, you can tell by just looking at someone if you would take a check from them or not.

The truth is, everyday people are sometimes financially ignorant, and *you* have to pay the price.

Nearly everyone has bounced a check before for whatever reason. I am not exempt from that list. One year around the holidays, I had so many people bounce checks with me that it caused one of my checks to bounce. After that happened, I no longer would assume my deposits were clear for spending until two weeks after the deposit was made. Talk about inconvenience!

Regarding bad checks, you'll see plenty of them. No matter how honest a customer might seem, like I said before, nearly everyone bounces a check in his or her lifetime. Bad checks cost you money. Sure, you can follow through with the typical collection procedures and maybe get your money. But it will cost you valuable time, your bank's return check fees, and a huge headache. If you don't collect the money yourself, you will have to hire a company to do it for you. Those companies won't guarantee collection, and if they do collect the money their commission is 50 percent of the check's face value.

If you have a seemingly un-collectable debt with one of your customers, you have the option of taking that customer to court to try and get a judgment in your favor. But there will be court fees associated with your case and most likely you will need legal representation, which could be very expensive.

Credit card machines are very convenient for any payments. As soon as the card clears for the sale, the money is as good as in the bank. But those machines cost you. You buy the machine or rent it monthly. For each transaction you are charged a flat fee and a percentage of the sale. In total, I found the cost to be around 5 percent of the sale. With some customer "cash back" cards you are charged an additional percentage.

Be careful when ordering your credit card machine. It boosts sales, and it's a sure thing on payments, but it can be costly. Personally, I like cash. Who doesn't?

How Many Lawyers Does It Take?
— Lawsuits —

Scott Farlow, Fambiz, Inc., dba Sears, North Bend, Oregon — Working for myself, I feel very strange leaving the business to go away for a few days. There's a huge amount of stress worrying about how we're doing. I worry about if someone comes into my store and falls and breaks their leg or something. It goes through my mind constantly. But when I worked for someone else, those things were not really a concern for me because I was not responsible for them. I didn't have to worry about someone else's security or safety, or about someone suing my business or me personally. I now have to protect that investment I have, it's stressful.

This is a true story. A family went to the local county park for a day of fun. The husband drank liquor all day. When he was good and smashed, he decided he wanted to rent a rowboat from the concessionaire at the park. He was refused service because of his intoxication. When the clerk went inside his office, the drunken man went out on the dock, stole the rowboat, and started paddling out into the lake. The clerk quickly ran outside yelling at the man to return the boat at once. The man refused and stood up in the rowboat. He lost his balance and fell out into the lake and drowned. His family sued the park and concessionaire for four million dollars. The family won the lawsuit. How could they win, you ask? The reason they won the lawsuit was because they argued the rowboat should have been locked to the dock so a drunken person couldn't take the rowboat out into the lake.

Horse rentals are probably considered one of the highest risk businesses. Yet one of the worst lawsuits brought against me was not from a horse injury at all. It was from an eighty-five-year-old woman. When I built a tack store at my ranch, the city required me to put in a twenty-foot handicap ramp along side the steps to the patio that led to the store entrance. The old woman went down the steps instead of using the handicap ramp. She missed the step and fell. She hit her head on the handrail, which she admitted she was not holding on to. She tried to sue me for her missing the step. I won the suit, but the hassle and bad mark with the insurance company were not good. When you have claims with your insurance carrier, win or lose, it's *not* going to help keep your rates down.

> **The myth is, you won't need any insurance in your type of business.**

> **The truth is, in our world today people are just not held responsible for their own actions — you are — so get enough insurance.**

If a customer slips on your floor and hurts themselves, even if the floor wasn't slick, but rather they were wearing loose slippery bottom shoes — they'll own you. Unfortunately, that's the way it is nowadays.

Make sure you carry enough liability insurance along with your other insurances. It might someday save your business, your home, and all of your other valuable property. Also, you should look into an LLC (limited liability corporation) if you are in a risky business. It separates your personal assets from your business. You can set this up yourself or an attorney can talk to you more about this and other options, and if you will need them to protect yourself.

5

"How Long Will it Take?"

You Want it When?
— Time Frame —

We live in a world of "I wants," and worse than that, we want it now. Technology gives us everything we want at the touch of a button. We have Internet access to find any tidbit of information we could possibly want or need. But we are so impatient waiting for a download that we are willing to pay up to sixty dollars a month just to get faster Internet access. It probably adds up to a buck a minute, but by golly, we get it fast! We have no patience left in our society — it's move out of the way, or get trampled. When starting a new business, patience is the key. It takes a long time to get from A to Z. Most often people want to go straight to "L," for the "Life of luxury" instead of stating at "A," Assessing the market, "B," Being financially prepared, "C," Committing to time investment, and on through Z.

You can't rush growth. You need good ideas and a good product that will sell. When you have that, along with a good business plan, growth will happen, and you go along for the ride just steering the car. Take advantage of that Internet access to research your product or idea, but don't rush the process. Yield to the yellow lights, and don't run through the stop signs.

The time it will take for your business to show signs of being successful can vary. Some new businesses show profits early on. But generally, it's a very slow process and requires the owner to be patient and have a personal commitment to work hard.

The myth is, you plan on hiring people to do most of the work.

The truth is, you are not entitled to success, it is earned, and earning it takes time — your time.

Money doesn't grow on trees, and it certainly didn't grow there for successful business owners. Everyone has to earn it. Everyone starts somewhere, and generally it's at the bottom.

Your ultimate goal may be the same as many people hope for — to have someone else doing all the work. But when you start out, you will be the one setting up your sales and you will be the one putting in all the hours — there's no way around that. If you are successful, and you are able to find great employees, eventually you might be able to put yourself in that laid back position.

James K. Flanagan, Prado Equestrian Center, Chino, California — Put your goals at an even perspective so you can feel good about yourself by making them. Keep them realistic and make small short-term goals as well as long-term goals.

They call it "small business" for a reason. You're not likely to make millions of dollars in small business. If you choose a business with unlimited potential for growth and income, over a period of time — usually years — you might find that million-dollar bankroll, but either way, these things take time. Of all the business owners I interviewed, the average time working in their business from the first day to showing a dollar profit was three and a half years. To derive this average I listed each of their "years to show profit" and deleted the lowest and the highest numbers. Then I divided the remaining total number by the number of remaining businesses. That makes three and a half years a realistic estimate of how long it might take you to show a profit. Of course, some will take longer and some will take less, but it gives you a good idea of what to plan for.

Abigail Ashworth, Personal Touch Of Hair Design, Blackwell's salon, Coos Bay, Oregon — In hair design, it's going to take you about two years just to build up a clientele to where you're making a living wage. It just takes time.

The time it takes you to be successful will also depend on how much time you're willing to invest and how successful you want to be. The more time you can invest, the more quickly you might reach a successful level.

> Rick Gitchen, Seattle's Best Coffee®, Chino Hills, California — We were actually profitable from day one, but my brother and I both worked seven days a week for the first year.

Am I Rich Yet?
— Profits and Loss —

Showing profits and making money are two totally different things in business. You can make a million bucks, but if your expenditures are that or above, you haven't made s—! In fact, you're probably sinking quickly into debt.

The myth is, if you're only paying one dollar for your item and you can sell it for two dollars, your profit is one dollar.

The truth is, there are costs involved with selling that item. Showing a profit can take years in any type of business.

Joe Benetti, Benetti's Italian Restaurant, Coos Bay, Oregon — I had the grandeur ideas that everyone else thinks — that there will be a lot of money when you go into business. You just open the doors and everything that comes in is yours. Well that wasn't the case and so I wasn't making anything. It was a good thing I didn't have to pay myself minimum wage cause I would have been in deep trouble. There was no way I could have done that. I actually began to make a profit after the fifth year.

Restaurants used to make about 15 percent of their gross receipts, now if they make 10 percent, they're doing well. The laws nowadays are so difficult. Employee laws, licensing laws — they make it difficult to operate at a profit.

Big companies are not exempt to breaking even or losing money. In 2005, of all the big airline companies in business, Southwest Airlines was the only airline to show a profit.

Understand that what goes in, must come out in order to break even. Then it must come out above that to show a profit. Believe it or not, some people just don't get that!

Joan Marangio, F.M. Co. Boutique, Ontario, California — It took me three years to show a profit because I had to learn what to buy and sell.

Roberta Abel, Giftabel.com, Coos Bay, Oregon — I've learned that drop shipping from the wholesaler saves me from having to keep a lot of products in stock. When I get the order, I just fax it or e-mail it to my supplier and they ship it directly to my customer. Then I have a merchant account that allows them to deposit the money directly into my bank account. I just handle the order a little bit and I make more profit with less work. That should be your goal.

If you are consistent and accurate with your bookkeeping, it should appear very clear to you whether or not you are showing a profit or loss. I believe everyone is capable of keeping and balancing their own books in a small business. But as your business grows, you might want to hire a bookkeeper to help keep the extra work to a minimum for you.

Jim Pionke, Ace and Bubba Treasure Hunters, Racine, Wisconsin — If you wouldn't be willing to do it on a break-even basis, you're really going to be disappointed after about two years. We broke even after three years.

Once you start earning enough profit to survive, you should start looking for extra profit to reinvest into your business to maintain it properly and expand.

> Joe Benetti, Benetti's Italian Restaurant, Coos Bay,
> Oregon — I am constantly putting money back into
> the restaurant, whether it's new equipment, redoing
> the floors, or redoing the kitchen.

Starting your own business can have terrific tax benefits. Everything you buy to start-up and operate your business is tax-deductible, but you should prepare yourself for what happens when you start showing those profits. I strongly suggest you set up monthly, or quarterly, estimated tax payments through your tax consultant as soon as you start your business to avoid any surprises at the end of the year. Keep good records and receipts of all your expenses to get the most deductions possible by law. Remember this: if it turns out that you owe money to the IRS, you *will* be charged interest on it.

You've Done It
— Defining Success —

Success depends on your own definition of the word. In your own life now, only you can personally define success.

> Dan Abel, AD Construction and Remodel, LLC, Coos
> Bay, Oregon — I feel like my bills are paid and I can
> spend time with my family and still get work done,
> then I am successful. But that's this week — next week

I could be miserable and failing! But I figure, I'm still here and I'm still standing. So I guess I'm successful.

> Asked to the contractor:
> *"What would you do if you won the lottery?"*
> Contractor's reply:
> *"I'd keep doing my work until
> I spent that money too!"*

If you have a beautiful family, a loving, supportive husband or wife, and great kids, you probably consider yourself successful, right? If you went out and purchased your first home, fixed it up, and finally quit paying rent on a dump apartment, you were successful, right? Whenever we set a goal in our lives, we work hard to reach that goal. Success is not free — you have to have a goal and a vision and the passion to get there. Business is like a marriage. A marriage takes time, devotion, commitment, and a lot of hard work. Your business will require the same effort. How you define success will help you set your short and long term goals.

Do you want to start your business as a sideline for a little extra cash, or are you looking to be the next Donald Trump?

The myth is, you'll make a million dollars before you're 35.

The truth is, the bigger the goal, the longer the journey becomes to achieve success.

Only 25 percent of business owners are able to earn their *total* personal income from their business. Most (67 percent) earn their *primary* source of income through their business, those numbers are less for women. One third of businesses show a loss every year. What would you have to earn to feel successful?

Asked to the contractor:
"What would you do differently to be more successful?"
Contractor's reply:
"Go into another line of work!"

Rick Gitchen, Seattle's Best Coffee®, Chino Hills, California — To me success is having started something where there was nothing. Building something that now not only supports both my partner's families and mine, but also helps to support seventy-five employees and their families. Every one of my vendors counts on me to help support their business, which supports their families. It's almost like a living creature that so many people derive the benefit from. To me, that's the definition of success.

You need to decide what you want out of this before you pursue it in order to define success.

When you do succeed, give back to the community who allowed you to be a part of their commerce. When I say give back, I mean contribute what you can to help others. That can be monetary gifts to local charitable organizations, gift certificates from your company for fundraising events in your local community, or even sponsoring a nonprofit charitable event at your place of business. You could join your local Chamber of Commerce or your local Kiwanis group. For contact information for these organizations see "other helpful Web addresses" in the back of this book. Giving back will make you feel good about yourself and your business. Look at it as a way to celebrate your success.

> Scott Farlow, Fambiz, Inc., dba Sears, North Bend, Oregon — I can't offer monetary donations because we're just not financially set yet, but I don't say no to anyone. I'll always find things to donate for gift baskets and such. You have to do something, because without your community you're nothing.

> Abigail Ashworth, Personal Touch of Hair Design, Blackwell's Salon, Coos Bay, Oregon — If you want the community to support you, you have to support your community.

Tired Yet?
— Retirement —

Well you've made it to the big time! You have done it — you're your own boss! Now, how will you retire? If you plan to retire someday from this new business venture you've started, you need to plan now. Most new entrepreneurs are so busy starting up and operating their business that they never think much about retirement. Retirement is eventually something you'll most likely need. Only 2 percent of business owners are able to offer retirement benefits to their employees, so how many business owners do you think have their own plan? I can tell you, not many. Most business owners I spoke with either had no plan or hoped retirement would just happen somehow.

> Dan Abel. AD Construction and Remodel, LLC, Coos Bay, Oregon — My plan for retirement is to die early so my wife can cash in on my insurance policy! But honestly, I have to say, like so many others in my trade, we have no retirement plan.

Some business owners who owned their business's building or location felt that the equity in that real estate would be sufficient to retire on. They might be right, but what if you don't own that building? This is the time to plan. New business owners need to take responsibility for their own future, not just the next year or so. You no longer work for someone else, which means there's no paycheck and no retirement plan. When you're counting your profits, you should always consider what you need to save out of that money: health insurance costs, business insurance, and retirement.

The myth is, you can run your company for ten years and then retire.

The truth is, a large percentage of business owners never reach retirement.

> Abigail Ashworth, Personal Touch Of Hair Design, Blackwell's Salon, Coos Bay, Oregon — It's harder for people who are self-employed because you not only have to fund your own retirement, but you have to fund your own life while you're doing that. You have to plan and do your own IRA and you have to do your own saving.

So let's say you do plan ahead and your retirement day comes, how will you feel about all that free time? Believe it or not, some people get so accustomed to working long hours every day that they can't see themselves retiring. Some people get bored and don't know what to do with themselves. I found there really is a new life out there, without a job, and it's not scary or boring at all. When you begin your financial plan for retirement, you should also think of things you could do when you get there. Many of the things you enjoy get put on the back burner when you become self-employed. When you retire, you get back the opportunity to do those things again. For myself, I was so exhausted from years of hard work and worry that I never got bored and I pursued my hobbies (and slept a bunch!). You could also volunteer your time to a worthy charitable organization — it's a rewarding experience.

"Being The Boss"

Words From the Big Cheese

The myth is, you won't have any problem telling someone what to do.

The truth is, it's never as easy as you think to be the boss.

Small business in this country employs more people than all of the Fortune 500 companies combined.

When potential business owners were asked why they wanted to start their own business, the largest percentage of them answered, "I want to be my own boss." We all fantasize about being the "big cheese," but in reality it is a very tough position. Sometimes you'll feel like the whole world falls on your lap.

In my business I didn't have many employees, but a few of my full-timers were the sole financial providers for their families. It made me feel somewhat responsible for them. If I had to let them go for whatever reason, I would be left feeling like I had let their families down, not just one person. It's hard enough to be responsible for your own family's well being, but when you hold the key to other people's well being, it's tougher yet.

> Scott Farlow, Fambiz, Inc., DBA Sears, North Bend, Oregon — Having people working for me is the hardest part of my job. I enjoy it, but with thirteen people working for you, every one of them has a different personality to deal with.

> James J. Flanagan, Prado Equestrian Center, Chino, California — It's scary at times, and lonely at times. It can be a real challenge.

> Dan Abel, AD Construction and Remodel, LLC, Coos Bay, Oregon — I feel pretty good about being the boss; it's in my nature and I like to control the situation. But I hate to fire someone.

> Joe Benetti, Benetti's Italian Restaurant, Coos Bay, Oregon — I like being the boss, I just sometimes don't like everything that comes with it. Sometimes it's overwhelming.

Abigail Ashworth, Personal Touch Of Hair Design, Coos Bay, Oregon — I wasn't good as the boss. I just wanted someone to come in and do the work and I wouldn't have to tell them what to do, but that wasn't the way it worked.

Rick Gitchen, Seattle's Best Coffee®, Chino Hills, California — It's about the relationship. People need to feel as if they belong when they work in a place; they need to feel ownership. People are counting on you. When I sign a check that goes to supporting their family, that's gratifying to me.

Sandy Flanagan, Prado Equestrian Center, Chino, California — How I feel about being the boss depends on the day. If it's a good day, people like what you're doing, it's great.

When we work for someone else we have set responsibilities and we do our job. But often we see our boss doing another job that looks easier than ours. If we could walk in their shoes, would we want to? Standing back always paints a prettier picture than being close up. Our boss probably has his job because he worked harder than the other guy to get it. Maybe it is easier, but I believe unless we are working side by side all day long with our boss, we don't know for sure.

When you are the boss, most likely you will be looked upon as having the *easy* job. Nobody will notice the amount of hours you put in, the grueling paperwork, the sleepless nights of worry, or the stress on your family. You will always be looked at as the one with the easy job and all the money.

Being the big cheese isn't always as glamorous as it is made out to be. Being fair and honest with people can make the position more comfortable for you. Always remember, the people who work for you are what keep you in business. Take care of your good employees.

So that's it in a nutshell, the real truth about self-employment. The fact that you even read this whole book shows your desire is genuine.

Now retake the quiz from the beginning of this book and see how your answers compare.

Yes   No

[   ]   [   ] Do I have enough cash to invest (other than necessary household income)?

List where your business assets will be coming from:

[   ]   [   ] Do I have enough household income or savings to get me through the first year?

Where is your monthly household income coming from?

[   ]   [   ] Am I good with my personal financial management?

List any late payments you've had in the past five years:

[   ]   [   ] Will I have medical insurance for my family and myself?

Where will it come from and what will the cost be?

[   ]   [   ] Am I in good health? When was your last physical?

Yes   No

[   ]   [   ] Do I have adequate knowledge or education in the business field I am choosing? List all experience and education;

[   ]   [   ] Is there room in the market I have chosen for additional competitors? Who is your competition?

[   ]   [   ] Do I have unlimited time to invest?
What are your other commitments?

[   ]   [   ] Do I have patience? Ask your spouse or mother!

[   ]   [   ] Does my family support me in this business venture, 100 percent? List any who are skeptical:

Yes   No

[   ]   [   ] Do I get along well with other people?

[   ]   [   ] Am I committed to and excited about this business venture?

Once you've read this book, and maybe several others, if the numbers don't add up for you, but every instinct you have tells you that the numbers are wrong, you're probably better off to go ahead with your business idea. Because as long as you haven't got much to lose, you will probably always regret not trying. Remember this, businesses don't fail — people do.

The Outcome
"My Final Story"

In 1986, I bought a losing horse ranch in California. It took me only two years to break even, but I spent years building the ranch up from there. I tore down that old office after the first year and built a new, bigger office and porch. I turned part of the new office into a store, selling horse supplies to my boarders. A few years later, I added another 1,000 square feet to the office and I opened a bigger store. The store was the first leg from my spider core.

Originally, there were only seven private boarded horses there. Little by little I fixed up the twenty-five old corrals and added several more. After two years there were fifty horses boarded, after eight years there were ninety, and by my twelfth year in business, I was boarding over one hundred twenty privately owned horses.

I added pony rides for the public on my second year. After my fifth year, I added a string of twelve hourly rental horses. Another leg.

Early on, my dad said something to me that I laughed off. He said, "It's not the dollars you make and save, it's the nickels, dimes, and quarters." My first thought was, "What a dummy — of course it's the dollars." But I realized soon after, he was right. It is the small things that add up. Sometimes I think the nickels, dimes, and quarters from adding a snack and soda machine for my customers was what kept me afloat in those early years. The machines were a short but important leg of my spider.

Over time, I added more amenities to the ranch. New customers wanted more for their money. I added a barn, several riding arenas, a hay shelter, pasture areas, horse bathing areas, and much more. I started hosting horse shows and fun days for other local horse owners. I even held annual fundraisers at my ranch for local charities.

I'd like to say the place grew like crazy. But the truth is, these things took years to develop and it was a hard journey. I managed to keep a good relationship with my clients over the years and most of them felt as if the ranch was their second home. Some of them would volunteer to help with improvements. Never underestimate the value of good volunteers. If I had not had the volunteer help of my clients at times, I would have gone nowhere. Those people took stock in the ranch and wanted it to be the best. My average boarder stayed with me for two and a half years — that's a good average in the horse boarding business. I had boarders that stayed the entire time I owned the ranch. I watched some of my customers' kids go from awkward fourth graders to college graduates. I even saw some of them grow up, marry, and start families of their own. I was so lucky to have had that experience. There was a reason my clients stayed as long as they did. I personally believe it was good customer service and commitment.

There were many sacrifices in my business. I worked seven days a week, 365 days a year, and averaged ten hours a day for the first six years. But after a few years, I was able to take time off for holidays and short vacations. Because of the type of business I chose, my daughter was able to spend her time at the ranch and I didn't have to miss out on sharing her childhood years. That was a great advantage for both of us.

When my health took a bad turn due to working outdoors in the heat and the everyday stress of running a business, it was time to walk away. I had grown a successful business. I made a deal to lease the ranch with a payment of about half my normal income, so I downsized my life and retired.

I owned and operated my horse ranch for fifteen years. I've only this year begun to realize what I built. People always say to me they admire what I did. But it wasn't until I was away from it for a couple years, that I realized how special it was. When I look back now, I am extremely proud of the business I built. Do I feel successful? Yes I do. You might be asking, was it worth it? Would I recommend it? When I think about the freedom it affords me now in my life, yes, it was well worth it. Will it be worth it to you? I can't answer that for you. Take what you have learned from this book and I know you can pursue your dream with fewer mistakes than me.

I now live happily in Oregon spending my days relaxing and enjoying my free time. I am again free to pursue any hobbies and dreams I have. But for right now, and because I can and because I've earned it, I think I'll just sit here and watch the sunset.

RECOMMENDED READING

Business Plans Made Easy, Mark Henricks and John Riddle
Entrepreneur Press, 2002

The Complete Small Business Sourcebook, Carl Hausman
and Wilbur Cross
The Stonesong Press, Inc., 1998

How to Soar Like an Eagle in a World Full of Turkeys, Robert
Stevenson
Seeking Excellence Publishing, 1997

The Nordstrom Way, Robert Spector and Patrick D. McCarthy
John Wiley and Sons, Inc., 2005

Small Time Operator, Bernard B. Kamoroff, CPA
Bell Springs Publishing, 2004

HELPFUL FEDERAL GOVERNMENT WEB ADDRESSES

Small Business Administration: www.sba.gov

Small Business Development Centers: www.sba.gov/sbdc

Department of Commerce: www.doc.gov

Department of Labor: www.dol.gov

Patent Office: www.uspto.gov

Trademark Office: www.uspto.gov

Copyright Office: www.lcweb.loc.gov/copyright

Customs Service: www.customsustreas.gov

Department of Transportation: www.dot.gov

Environmental Protection Agency: www.epa.gov

Federal Trade Commission: www.ftc.gov

Food and Drug Administration: www.fda.gov

Internal Revenue Service: www.irs.gov

Census Bureau: www.census.gov

Federal Government: www.business.gov

If one of the above addresses is invalid or for all other United States government sites go to: www.fedworld.gov

STATE GOVERNMENT WEB ADDRESSES

For your state government Website: www.state.[your state's two-letter abbreviation].us

OTHER HELPFUL WEB ADDRESSES

Chamber of Commerce: www.chamberofcommerce.com

Kiwanis Club: www.kiwanis.org

American Home Business Association: www.homebusiness.com

National Foundation of Women Business Owners: www.nfwbo.org

International Franchise Association: www.franchise.org

Sears Stores: www.searsdealerstores.com

Robert Stevenson: www.robertstevenson.org

Giftabel: www.giftabel.com

My Commitment To You!

This book was written to help people who have a desire to become self-employed. As the author of this book, I am responsible for the information provided. If you have any questions regarding starting up, or operating your new business, please feel free to visit my website at www.plainandsimplebooks.com or e-mail me at cdenbow@plainandsimplebooks.com

NAMES AND
TITLES INDEX